Wednesday's Children

Wednesday's Children

Adult Survivors of Abuse Speak Out

SUZANNE SOMERS

Putnam/HealingVision Publishing
New York

Published by G. P. Putnam's Sons   Putnam/HealingVision Publishing
Publishers Since 1838
200 Madison Avenue
New York, NY 10016

The author acknowledges permission to reprint
material from the following sources:

"I Am Your Child," written by Barry Manilow and Marty Panzer
© 1973 Careers-BMG Music Publishing, Inc. and SwaneeBravo! Music.
All Rights Reserved. Used by Permission.

"Broken Toys," © 1984 Sixteen Stars Music/BMI, Gloria Thomas
Music/BMI, administered by Copyright Management, Inc., and
Music Corporation of America/BMI. All Rights Reserved.
International Copyright Secured. Used By Permission.

"Four Quartets," from *The Complete Poems and Plays*
by T.S. Eliot, copyright 1943 by T.S. Eliot and renewed
1971 by Esme Valerie Eliot, reprinted by permission
of Harcourt Brace Jovanovich, Inc. and Faber & Faber, Ltd.

"Raindrops Keep Fallin' on My Head" Lyric by Hal David   Music by Burt
Bacharach   Copyright © 1969 Blue Seas Music, Inc., Jac Music Co., Inc. and
WB Music Corp. International Copyright Secured   All Rights Reserved

Library of Congress Cataloging-in-Publication Data
Somers, Suzanne.
Wednesday's children : adult survivors of abuse speak out/
Suzanne Somers.
p. cm.
ISBN 0-399-13743-2 (alk. paper)
1. Adult child abuse victims—United States—Case studies.
I. Title.
HV6626.5.S66 1992   92-8688 CIP
362.7'6—dc20

Designed by Rhea Braunstein

Printed in the United States of America
2 3 4 5 6 7 8 9 10

This book is printed on acid-free paper.

Monday's child is fair of face,
Tuesday's child is full of grace,
WEDNESDAY'S CHILD IS FULL OF WOE,
Thursday's child has far to go,
Friday's child is loving and giving,
Saturday's child works hard for a living,
But the child that's born on Sabbath day,
Is blithe and bonny and good and gay.

To my mother,
to my husband,
and to Bruce

Recovery is like an onion;
you peel away layer by layer,
each section bringing you
closer to clarity.
Along the way you cry a lot;
but when you finally reach
the center, the core,
you'll find it's really sweet.

ACKNOWLEDGMENTS

My deepest gratitude to all who supported me throughout this project.

Alan Hamel, my husband, for his continuing encouragement and love which kept me going through the overwhelming periods.

Phyllis Grann and Stacy Creamer for the idea.

Stacy Creamer, my editor extraordinaire, who showed me the way when I couldn't bear to part with a single word.

Marsha Yanchuck for scheduling and hours of typing. Also for giving "good phone."

Laurie Jacobson for her invaluable assistance the last few months. I could not have finished without her help.

Robert Schuster for the deal.

Gerry Myers for the information.

Arthur Weinthal for his wisdom.

Sheri Ferrand for her typing and typing and typing.

Caroline Somers, more typing.

Johann Sebastian Bach for providing the perfect background music.

And all the professionals—Robert Ackerman, Tim Allen, Claudia Black, John Bradshaw, Doug Braun, Cathleen Brooks, Jody Frank, Marti Heuer, Della Hughes, Jerry Moe, William Rader, Carol Trenery, Gary Weiss . . .

A special thank you to Dr. Timmen Cermak for writing the foreword.

CONTENTS

CONTENTS

*Problems call forth our
courage and our wisdom;
indeed, they create
our courage and our wisdom.
It is only because of problems
that we grow
mentally and spiritually.*

M. Scott Peck
The Road Less Traveled

INTRODUCTION

*T*HE keys to our adult selves are forged in childhood. The seed of self-esteem is planted through the steady love and care of a parent. But what if that parent is incapable of such steadiness or love? What if, through mental illness, alcoholism, drug abuse, separation, or just plain perversity, that parent sends a wrong signal to the child? What if that signal of love, so crucial to a happy child's development, is distorted or intermittent? What if there is no signal at all?

There are essentially three forms of child abuse: physical, sexual, and emotional. Physical abuse involves any form of striking a child or the threat of such violence. Sexual abuse involves touching or speaking to a child in a sexual way. Emotional abuse comes in many forms. There is the abuse of cruelty: harsh words, disparaging comments. There is the abuse of manipulation, where a parent uses any persuasive means available to see a child pursue a particular end. And then there is the emotional abuse of neglect.

If the consequences of these various forms of child abuse were uniform—if physical abuse in childhood resulted in behavior A in adulthood, sexual abuse resulted in behavior B, and emotional abuse in behavior C—we might have been clued into the damaging effects long before now. But different people can react altogether differently to the same form of abuse. One child who is beaten may internalize the violence, coming to believe that there is a logical reason for it: He must be bad and therefore deserving of such treatment. Another child faced with the very same beatings may harbor an ever-growing rage, a rage he may ultimately seek to quell with drugs or alcohol.

In my own case, growing up in an alcoholic home, I came to accept chaos as a normal state of affairs rather than the exception. I wound up sabotaging my first marriage simply because the calm left me unsettled and nervous; I had to create chaos where none existed because that's all I was familiar with.

As different as the responses to abuse can be, you'll soon recognize at least two threads of commonality.

First, abuse universally erodes self-esteem. Long after the bruises are healed and the yelling's stopped, people who've been abused feel they are worthless. That low self-esteem, that utter lack of self-worth propels people into choices in adult life that can only lead to unhappiness. Regaining self-esteem or gaining it where none ever existed seems to be key to any abused person's eventual recovery.

The other thread of commonality is the desire of those who've been abused to break the cycle. Again and again in the pages that follow you'll hear from people who are determined to raise their own children free of the kind of abuse and terror they themselves knew as kids.

Facing your demons, the realities of your childhood, is the first crucial step in recovery. Once you've acknowledged the hard facts of your early years, you can begin to appreciate how much that experience has shaped your behavior and mindset far into adulthood. But coming to terms with the truth is only a first step. I didn't realize that completely when I wrote the story of my life as the child of an alcoholic, *Keeping Secrets*. Back then I thought that simply naming the demons was enough. It was a vital first step, but for me recovery only began with that acknowledgment. It was the start of a long journey, one I'm still on today. Ingrained habits don't vanish with the simple realization of their cause. The more I could see how much my adult behavior was a product of growing up in an alcoholic home, the less I remained a prisoner to it.

So why this book? First, we need to get these issues out in the open. Child abuse—be it physical, sexual, or emotional—thrives in secret. As long as the perpetrators feel their actions will go unacknowledged and undetected, they will persist. They won't seek help. And their victims will remain without a voice, powerless against the torment, doomed to lives shaped by abuse.

Second, and more to the point, this book is about recovery, about freeing yourself from the legacy of an abusive past. It's bad enough if your childhood was tarnished by an abusive parent; worse still if the rest of your life continues to be shaped—or warped—by that experience.

In meetings of Alcoholics Anonymous, individuals in recovery give "qualifications" before the group. They tell what it was like when they were drinking, what happened to make them want to try to give it up a day at a time for good, and what it's like now that they're in recovery. Quite literally, they are telling their fellow recovering alcoholics what qualifies them for the program of AA.

Each chapter of *Wednesday's Children* is intended to serve as such a qualification, but instead of alcoholism, the issue is abuse. Each contributor shares what abuse he or she suffered in childhood, where that abuse led in adult life, and how he or she is trying to cope now.

In recovery programs, listeners are encouraged to identify with the speaker, not compare. That means they're to identify with the feelings the speaker expresses, not necessarily the actual particulars of his or her experience.

I encourage you to read these chapters in this same frame of mind. You may not have grown up where these people grew up. You may not have been treated in exactly the same abusive way. But however you were treated, you may feel the way these people felt at the hands of such abuse. You may have responded the same way in adulthood. If the personal stories here strike a chord in you, then this book will have served its purpose. And you'll be on your way to that important first step of recovery.

During the last two years I spent many hours with each person in this book, experiencing a whole gamut of emotions. Many times I wept along with them because the emotions were so raw. It was extremely painful going over and over all the feelings, the fear, and the heartache that comes from revealing the truth about oneself and those one loves the most. It takes a lot of courage. These people have done so for you.

I am grateful to all who participated in this book. I have removed my questions because they seemed intrusive. I have tried wherever possible to preserve the language the participants themselves used to describe reactions, feelings, and emotions.

Those in this book have offered their stories to prove they are happier today because they have taken the time to understand the effects abuse has had upon their lives. They were generous enough to go public with their innermost thoughts and feelings because they recognize that by sharing, others may be led out of their suffering and despair.

Few people are brave enough to dig this deep, but those who have taken the journey are rewarded with the inner peace that only comes from searching. I thank all the people in this book for sharing so openly and honestly. They welcomed me into their homes and shared their privacy. This book belongs to all of them— and I appreciate their trust in me to tell their stories. We hope that together we can impact change, provide a deeper understanding of abuse, and make a contribution.

In *Wednesday's Children* you'll find the stories of both famous and not-so-famous people. Famous or not, each contributor's reason for being here will become quite clear in the telling of his or her story. Just read each chapter and try to identify with the feelings expressed, not just the particulars.

Why the celebrities? Recently a reporter from *Newsweek* called to ask me if I could help her understand why so many celebrities were telling all. Was it for publicity's sake? Revenge maybe? What happened to the old adage, "Don't air your dirty laundry in public"?

From the reporter's tone, I could sense a backlash coming. Are celebrities who've spoken out on a range of taboo issues—substance abuse, incest—now going to be the fodder for ridicule and mockery?

I hope not. I believe Americans, for whatever reasons, feel more comfortable addressing personal problems of their own once celebrities they admire go public, owning up to experiencing those very same problems themselves. Alcoholism and drug abuse are good cases in point. Certainly the rising tide of interest in recovery from substance abuse has been steadily boosted by celebrities who have gone public about their own battles with alcohol and drugs.

Years ago, movie studios hired publicity men to write about their stars. Fans were treated to fabricated accounts of stars' glamorous lives and exotic pasts. *Her mother was a Russian princess; his father, a French count.* Never, ever, did you read that any of these stars came from troubled homes. Never was there any mention of abuse in any form. Every bit of "fact" to reach the public was as glossy as the stars' publicity stills.

I'm thankful that we live in a time when that gloss can come off our celebrities. Maybe that *Newsweek* reporter would relish a return to the old days, but not me. I only wonder what my life might have been like if the adult stars of my childhood days had told the truth about their lives. Maybe I wouldn't have grown up thinking I was the only girl in America with a father like mine living in a household like mine. The sense of isolation was fierce—and one more reason for me to keep silent about our problem.

My feeling is, let's get these issues on the table. Let's clear the air. Let's share our experience, strength, and hope with each other. Only if victims of abuse feel their stories will be treated credibly will they muster the courage to step forward into the light.

A final word: this book is not about blame. Blame doesn't serve any useful purpose. Blame enables us to stay the way we are and remain victims. Blame is a cover-up for shame. When you blame someone else, you don't have to deal with your own feelings of shame. What's more, people who abuse children were more likely than not abused themselves—and by people who were themselves abused. What we're dealing with are victims of victims of victims . . .

Wednesday's Children is about telling the truth, about speaking honestly and openly about very painful experiences. But the aim of this truth-telling is self-discovery. It's not about your parents, it's about you. It's about the rest of your life and how you're going to live it. It's time to face the truth, then let go and move on. An abusive parent may have owned your early years, but you own the rest of them—at least you can. It's up to you to pry yourself away from the legacy. You do not have to remain a hostage to your childhood. You do not have to live life as a victim. It's up to you to break the cycle. I hope this book will be a start.

Dictionaries define ABUSE as:

to use wrongly or improperly; misuse
to treat in a harmful, injurious, or offensive way
to speak insultingly or harshly
to assult physically
wrong or improper use
misuse of privileges
improper treatment; maltreatment
physically harmful treatment
corrupt practice or custom; offense
language that condemns or villifies, usually unjustly, intemperately,
    and angrily

Abuse implies an outburst of harsh and scathing words against
    another—*often one who is defenseless.*

FOREWORD

Timmen L. Cermak, M.D.

*W*HEN I invited a professional colleague to a conference on adult children of alcoholics, his initial impression was that much of what he heard was anecdotal and exhibitionistic. "I don't understand everyone's compulsion to talk so openly about the details of their own lives," he said. This will be the same response many people have to *Wednesday's Children,* and it is important to explain how this reaction misses the point.

It may be true that no collection of stories or anecdotes *proves* anything scientific. But rarely does scientific research have the emotional impact which lies within the human stories in this important book. Child abuse happens one child at a time, and is faced alone by each victim. The question should not be, "Why are they compelled to tell their stories?" but rather, "Why doesn't our country feel compelled to listen to their stories?" The underlying theme of this book is the listening that Suzanne Somers is doing (and each reader is reinforcing). The events being recorded are not simply people telling about their lives, but rather our *listening* as they share their histories.

The message winding its way through these pages is that silence is deadly. The universal human impulse is to deny abuse, whether you perpetrated it or suffered it. But the price of silence and denial is far too great. Each story tells us that emotional freedom depends upon breaking the bonds of silence. To gain this freedom, the victims of abuse must find the courage to speak truthfully about their experience. One of the primary sources of their courage is our willingness to listen. This is the most important contribution we can make to the safety needed to deal with the excruciating realities of their lives.

Is it embarrassing for you to hear people speak of incest, physical abuse from a parent, and their own misguided efforts to keep from speaking by using alcohol, other drugs, and sex to quell the inner turmoil? Is it uncomfortable to hear the anger that can linger throughout adult life after a child has been emotionally battered? Do you wish all this would go away? Is there an urge to find reasons why people should remain silent? (After all, these people profit from getting publicity any way they can find it, don't they?)

It is normal to find yourself shying away from their stories of abuse. But all of them are telling us that they tried shying away from their own stories as well, and it only compounded the problem. Remaining silent is precisely what the perpetrators of abuse want their children to do, almost invariably because the perpetrators know that something is wrong and are terrified themselves. When we promote silence, we continue the trauma. ("Is there *no one* to listen, to care!" the child wails. "There *is* no one who will ever listen," they come to believe. "I am bad for wanting to speak," they often conclude.)

Life can be brutal and violent for some of us; it has always been that way. Nothing has been able to stop the tides of violence which engulf children in our country, in distant countries, in our times and in distant times. Are you ready to allow this fact to be your excuse for remaining stoic and passive? If so, then you have no right to criticize those victims of abuse who would speak out. They are alone and must do whatever they can to find solace on their own. If, on the other hand, you are not willing to be passive in the face of this ancient human scourge, then you will welcome their voices.

Is the time right, today, in America, to find ways to end this blight on the human soul? Can we possibly find ways to hear Cain's anger and disappointment without waiting until Abel is slain? Is it possible to embrace him and say gently but firmly, "Yes, Cain, you *are* your brother's keeper; and we are *all* brothers and sisters"?

Not all victims of child abuse are as eloquent as those recorded here. Many are nearly inarticulate, since they have yet to find anyone who will listen. Their silence has led to a muteness, and then a numbness of their souls. I think of a twenty-year-old boy I know, Richard, who is waiting to be tried for murder. When I met him, the only way I knew of his pervasive history of being abused was from the trail of police reports and court documents which his public defender had collected. When questioned about his past, he could not find many memories when he looked within himself. Those he did find were the myths which had been dictated to him by a doting grandmother. He had little awareness of the source of his rage and humiliation.

Richard grew up around almost continuous humiliation and physical threats from his wildly alcoholic father. He observed violence between his father and several stepmothers, including gashes in the scalp from an ax, broken bones, and visits by the SWAT team to disarm his raging father. He was kicked in the eye with a steel-toed boot and then told he was loved. The family went out to a steak house instead of to the hospital. There is no acceptable excuse for murder, except self-defense; and now Richard must face the consequences of his own rageful acts. He is likely to spend his life in prison, or be executed. We all suffer when children are abused and not listened to.

I wonder whether our country has the will to listen long enough to hear the truth about child abuse. Everyone is caught in the same maelstrom when abuse occurs. Some are older and bigger. Others are younger and smaller. The older, bigger ones almost always experienced the same level of abuse when they were young and small; or else the chronic misuse of alcohol and other drugs is clouding their ability to see what they are doing. In either case, everyone is a victim in many ways. We must have the courage to react in the best way to whichever victims cross our paths and look longingly in our direction for help.

Approach each story as a longing glance in your direction. Suzanne Somers met that glance by sitting down and listening. That is the greatest help we can give.

27

Emotional Abuse

It never makes the headlines or the evening news; perpetrators never draw serious jail time for it. Nevertheless, emotional abuse can leave psychic wounds that run deep even if they are intangible. Sometimes subtle, sometimes brazenly overt, emotional abuse is easily the most widespread form of abuse. Parents who are neither physically nor sexually abusive to their children can abuse them emotionally. As Dr. Robert J. Ackerman, doctor and author of numerous books including *Perfect Daughters, Same House—Different Home,* and *Children of Alcoholics,* points out, physical and sexual abuse cannot exist independently of emotional abuse. By definition, physical and sexual abuse entail emotional abuse as well.

Ackerman divides emotional abuse into two categories: "There's emotional abuse and then there's emotional neglect—which is very different. Emotional abuse could be verbal belligerence. For example, if every time you talk to your parents about your aspirations they come back and tell you you're stupid, that's emotional abuse. That's a very belligerent, belittling statement. On the other hand, emotional neglect is not being able to meet the emotional needs of the child. This can be little things—never showing up for baseball games or refusing to listen—'You're too young to be depressed,' or 'Don't cry; it wasn't that bad.' In most abusive families both of those forms are going on."

In my own case, every time I told my dad my ambitions, he said

31

I was a big zero—that's emotional abuse. Emotional neglect is a more subtle, often unintentional form of abuse, an inability to meet the emotional needs of the child. Patti Davis is a perfect example of a child whose parents were emotionally unavailable to her. She is still angry about it and is still trying to get their attention. Ronald Reagan's father was an alcoholic. The family legacy trickles down.

Jerry Moe, Director of Children's Resources at Sierra Tucson in Arizona, says, "In the treatment field I was always trained that you help break through people's denial, but with little kids, denial is what allows them to survive. Denial can be a really powerful, wonderful thing. It lets children survive in spite of the fact that their parents are often emotionally unavailable to them. The most powerful picture a kid ever drew for me was from a little girl. I gave her papers and crayons and asked her to draw her family. On the middle of the page she drew a bottle as if it were six feet tall. The biggest creature on the page was the bottle and it had spaghetti-string arms and legs. At the stem of the bottle was a hideous face, a monster face. Right behind the bottle was a picture of the little girl's dad. This was a very creative little girl. She had her dad's hair flying all over the place, while one of his hands was just about to grab the stem of the bottle. Right behind Dad was a picture of her mom. Mom looked worried and concerned. She had one hand up just about to grab the back of Dad's collar as if to yank him away before he grabbed the bottle. Mom had on an apron, and holding on to the apron strings were the ten-year-old girl and her younger brother, and their feet weren't even on the ground; they were up in the air as if Mom was moving so fast that the kids' feet weren't even on the ground. That's the most powerful definition of a dysfunctional family system or addicted family system that I've ever seen. The kids go along for the ride and get involved as a result.

"The little girl looked at the picture and she really got angry. She got angry at the alcohol, then she got angry at her mom and dad. I mean really angry. 'Why do you do this? Why do you yell at me? Why are you never there? Why do you hit us? Why? Why? Why did I have to be in this kind of a family?' Once she was finished, then the tears came because what was behind the anger for this little girl was the shame; and when she got right into it, it was, 'What's wrong with me? What's wrong with me? I've tried everything. I've tried to bring home a good report card; I've tried to keep Mom and Dad happy; I've tried to stop them from fighting; and I tried to get Dad to come to my school things and not to go out and drink, and why? Why? Why? Why am I such a bad kid?' Once children begin to look at the pain and the loss, they immediately get into feelings and start to roll. There is now a space created for the kids to take a look at the whole picture and see what's really going on.

"It's sad that denial keeps little kids alive. They survive; but it's not until kids break through their denial that they're able to really understand that it's not their fault."

Growing up with emotional abuse is like trying to negotiate through a jungle.

In *Double Duty,* Claudia Black writes, "Emotional abuse is a constant fear of impending violence and the nervousness and unpredictability of never knowing what will happen next. Abused children cannot protect themselves physically, so they fight to protect themselves emotionally. They are frightened of showing their feelings. When children are physically attacked, it reinforces their feelings of low self-worth. It makes trusting others impossible. Anyone who has been abused has much to be sad and angry about. Abuse is a terrible violation. It is a blatant act of betrayal by those who are supposed to love and care for you. Abused children do not feel safe and protected."

Victims of emotional abuse sometimes become workaholics, alcoholics, or drug addicts. They have low self-esteem, feel isolated and lonely, have trouble with relationships and difficulty trusting people. They also experience depression and an overwhelming feeling of powerlessness.

If your parents screamed at each other most of the time—like Desi Arnaz, Jr.'s did—that becomes your model for relating to those around you. To Desi, that's how love was expressed. He grew up believing that jealousy and anger were how people showed that they cared.

Children who have been emotionally abused do not get their

proper nurturing. No one is saying the little things that give children their sense of value, the praise that naturally comes in a healthy home. "What a good report card," or "What a nice job you did cleaning your room," or "You look so nice today." These are the simple little everyday things that translate in the child's mind into, "I have worth; I am a good person; I am loved; I am valuable."

When a child is raised in an emotionally abusive home, the focus is not on the child. Everyone in the family walks on eggshells around the abusive parent in hopes of keeping him or her on an even keel. The family adapts to the abusive parent's moods. If he is happy, they can be happy; if he is upset, they will be upset. In this environment the children are learning their own needs and feelings are not important. They learn to live the parent's life, not their own. Life becomes painful and eventually these children will find some way to take their pain away. Some do this by overeating, some by becoming alcoholics or drug addicts, some do it with sex. Some take their pain away, as I did, by shopping and spending money they do not have, thus creating a crisis. In an emotionally abusive home, there is no one to reinforce the child's unique qualities; therefore, children with talent and special abilities often never realize their potential.

The regulations in these homes can become arbitrary and unfair. Sometimes the rules are impossibly rigid, as in the case of Gary Crosby. He was ordered to lose weight each week; if he did not fulfill his father's unreasonable expectations, he was beaten and verbally belittled.

Because of the alcoholism in my family, there were no rules, no boundaries. I wrongly thought no one cared where we were or what time we got home. Both of these examples translate equally to the child's mind: "No one cares about me." A feeling of worthlessness emerges.

We are powerfully shaped by our parents. Childhood is a crucial time in terms of development, learning trust, and gaining a sense of self-worth. If during childhood this growth doesn't occur, then the child matures physically into adulthood but without the proper coping skills and sense of self-esteem. Jerry Moe says, "The adult children movement is primarily about going back and reconnecting with that magical little boy or little girl inside that so many kids let go of in order to survive, in order to stay alive. When they don't have a chance to be kids, a lot of people grow up and get stuck in their incomplete and augmented development. In an addicted family, the child's own needs tend to get subordinated to meeting the needs of the family. It means they put their lives "on hold" and let go of the precious little boy or girl in order to survive." There's a vital need to go back and recapture that childhood, to learn all of the important developmental lessons that were overlooked the first time around, if the adult is to thrive and be happy.

Babies come into this world with a pure, clean slate. When children are emotionally abused, they are taught by their parents to conceal their feelings. They learn to ignore their real feelings and adapt. As they grow, ignoring those feelings becomes almost second nature. Such children feign indifference when they're emotionally hurt. They pretend to be attentive when they are disinterested. They sublimate past issues of abuse and the accompanying fear, humiliation, and shame. They repress painful memories. They adapt to make others happy. They learn to keep secrets—not only to protect others but also to insulate themselves. They push the pain away and refuse to acknowledge that it ever happened.

But feelings do not disappear; suppressed pain lies there smoldering at the bottom of our souls. Abused children pretend to be in control, never allowing themselves to dig below the surface. Then, when they least expect it, the pain emerges in a wide variety of forms.

I had no idea why I became crisis-oriented as an adult. I never made the connection to my crisis-riddled childhood. Cindy Williams never connected the stomach problems and constant nausea she suffered as a child to the terror she felt during her father's drinking binges. In her adult life today she is plagued by a "bad stomach" and ulcers.

Cheryl Crane invented a playmate, a companion to combat the loneliness and feelings of abandonment. Such a response is evident in many of the participants' stories. Cheryl says, "She was as real to me as if she really existed. She was my friend, my confidante, and my playmate. I don't remember the first day she was there. I just remember her being there. Maybe she was partially me. She had all the attributes I didn't have, and she helped me to survive. That's why I created her, although I didn't know it at the time. I trusted her. She appeared after a series of people left me.

"People always left me," Cheryl says: "It was frightening because there was never an explanation. I thought it was me. I blamed myself. Later, as I grew a little older, I would hear people arguing and then they would leave. I became totally afraid of anger. Anger would signify, 'Uh-oh. Somebody's going to be gone. Another person will leave.' The more I lost people as I went along, the more I closeted my emotions. I was afraid to get close to someone for fear they wouldn't be around. I clung even tighter to my grandmother because she seemed the one constant; she was there, and I made sure no one removed her from me."

Jerry Moe says, "Children of alcoholics always pick the wrong people to share things with because no one's ever given them a map of who safe people are. Often their parents have been the absolute antithesis of what safe people should be. Safe people don't laugh at children when they tell them about their problems or feelings. Safe people are people who won't blab it to everybody if they are told a confidence. Safe people are people who aren't always drinking and using drugs. Safe people are people who, when asked a question, don't put their heads in the newspaper and do other things; they look the child in the eye and really listen. Safe people are people who not only say they care but show it. They spend time with the child. They ask the child questions and listen to the child's answers. They are interested in the child's life. Safe people are people who can share *their* feelings. Safe people follow up on things. When they say they're going to do something for the child, they do it; and if they don't, they don't forget about it. They tell the child the reason why they couldn't and then they get to it later. Safe people are what healthy parents should be. If healthy parents are not an option, then kids need people who have most of these characteristics. Maybe an aunt to have in their lives, or their dad who is in recovery, or their grandma who lives across town. Or is it their next-door neighbor? Is it their bus driver? Is it their rabbi?

Their doctor? Their coach? Their scout leader? Knowing safe people empowers the children; they need to hook up to as many of these people in their lives as they can. Any one of these adults can help to reverse the effects of their abusive home. They need to know there are people they can turn to who truly care, instead of just stuffing it all inside and putting on that smile or that really quiet look or doing other things that do not let people see how they feel."

"A parent who is emotionally unavailable will negatively affect the child," says Marti Heuer. "Kids need attention. They thrive on attention. When they look in a parent's face, they desperately need to have reflected back to them acceptance, love, warmth, and caring. When they look in the eyes of that parent, they see what they are going to feel about themselves. If a parent has low self-esteem or is highly critical, then that child is going to see that in himself. He or she will walk away feeling shame. Children who grow up in a family with an angry parent might also grow up angry; or they could become quiet, withdrawn children intimidated by people who show any kind of anger. These children retreat within themselves because they are afraid of angry people. Unpredictability is scary to kids. If you look at alcoholic family systems, you might find different children in the same house taking on different roles because of their birth order. Some become little adults and some take on the role of the scapegoat. That is the really quiet kid in the family, who has decided, 'I don't want to do that. I don't want to act out and get kicked all over and be confronted. I'm not going to compete with my brother who's the model of the world and who's the best kid that there is. My choice is to be the quiet kid. Maybe I can just fade into the woodwork and nobody will notice me, then I'll be okay. I can survive that way.' We choose our roles. We survive based on what is already in front of us, and what we have to compare it to. Children have an amazing capacity on a subconscious level to watch and observe and figure out how they can adapt."

In my own life, I became a master at analyzing the level of tension in the house when I came home from school. I could smell if my dad was home and drinking. It was the combination of cigarettes and whiskey, a smell which to this day triggers an unpleasant feeling in me. I could tell by my father's posture and the angle of his eyelids how much he'd had to drink. I could tell by the back of his head how many drinks he'd had.

Cindy Williams says she could tell how much her father had been drinking by the way he drove his truck around the corner. Her life was focused on taking care of him. Angie Dickinson learned to shut out all her feelings to escape the verbal assaults of her father. Sally Marr, the mother of Lenny Bruce, cowered in fear from the onslaught of her mother's constant yelling and screaming.

Tim Allen, author of *Powerful Parents, Competent Kids*, says: "In some ways, our children say to us throughout their lives, 'I want to be treated with respect. I want you to take my ideas seriously. I want for you to listen to me and allow me to make my own decisions. But I do want your guidance and assistance. Sometimes I need it, even when I don't ask for it. I want to be free to decide how I am going to reach my goals. Give me the freedom to do that, please. Let me learn how. And if I don't quite make it, please don't jump down my throat for not getting it right the first time. And please don't call me stupid, dumb or worthless. Instead, explore with me the mistakes I make and encourage me to consider where things went wrong and how I might do things differently the next time. Let me come to my own conclusions, even if they differ from yours. All of this prepares me for when you're not there. If I rely on you to tell me the hows, the whys, and the whens of how to do things, then when I am on my own, I won't know how; I'm lost. Teach me how to be a part of a family and what relationships are all about. Teach me how to deal with relationships, with communication, with affection, and how what I do affects other people. If you teach me these things, I can take what you've taught me on to my other relationships—my school, my team, my family, my children. Teach me the art of negotiation, how to collaborate with others, how to argue effectively, and how to listen.' "

Growing up in an emotionally abusive home bears no resemblance to Tim Allen's description of a healthy parent-child interaction. It is the stuff of dreams to children in unhappy homes.

I remember longing for appropriate rules and boundaries. I

craved approval and encouragement and the right to fail without ridicule. Most children from emotionally abusive and/or neglectful homes have no way to comprehend a healthy relationship because the ones they know growing up are so dysfunctional. There is no preparation to coexist in society. There is no barometer for what is normal. They guess at normalcy and pretend to be happy, never piecing together the complex puzzle that would show them that the faulty patterns learned in childhood have followed them into adulthood and are the reason for the chaos in their lives.

Those things that hurt, instruct.

BENJAMIN FRANKLIN

SUZANNE SOMERS

*M*Y father never beat me. He never abused me sexually. But my early years were terror-filled. My father was a prisoner to his alcoholism, and in consequence, so were we, his family.

My father was drunk the day I was born. That's pretty much the way I remember him being for the next thirty-five years of my life. I have an older sister, Maureen, an older brother, Dan, and a younger brother, Michael. Maureen and Dan remember some of the good times. When I was a child, Dan often tried to comfort me by saying, "You know, before you were born, it wasn't always like this. We had friends over, we had parties." But I misunderstood. I thought he was trying to tell me that my arrival into this family had wrecked everything, so in my child's mind, with my lack of understanding, I felt responsible for all the family problems.

By the time I was born, my dad was well into "the hates." "The hates" are one of the stages of alcoholism. For as long as I could remember, my dad was filled with self-loathing. He hated being drunk, just hated it. I know he'd never planned to become a drunk, yet that's what he'd become. There had been a time in his life when he'd had a lot of potential. He'd had dreams and talent. He'd won a college scholarship during the Depression. He'd made All-City in baseball and was courted by professional teams. He was a feather-weight boxer and was scouted for the Olympics. He had so many opportunities, but instead wound up putting cases of beer on a boxcar for a living. Through booze, all those opportunities slipped away.

43

My dad turned a lot of his self-loathing outward. He'd show up drunk at school assemblies and shout obscenities at the nuns. I'd pretend not to hear what was happening. Sometimes during our priest's sermon at Sunday Mass, I'd hear my dad's unmistakable voice at the back of the church. He'd be talking too loud, calling the priest a dumb son-of-a-bitch. I knew the other worshipers could hear. I felt ashamed, as if his outbursts were my fault. It took away my dignity. I had this overwhelming feeling that I wasn't as good as other people. Even later, when things seemed to be going smoothly and I was feeling better about myself, I never knew when my dad might show up out of control and on a rampage.

My dad's outbursts weren't reserved for a public audience. We were the primary recipients. After a few hours of his nightly drinking, he'd get an attack of "the means." We wouldn't know what to expect, exactly, but it was never good. At the first signs of violence, we'd retreat to a closet upstairs that we'd set aside specifically for hiding. I remember that closet very well. It was a walk-in with enough room for all of us—me, Maureen, Dan, and my mother (Michael wasn't born yet)—to hide. Dan had rigged the lock on the inside of the door so even if Dad found us, he couldn't get in. Maureen, Dan, and my mother would sit on a cedar chest we had in there, leaning against each other to catch a little sleep. Next to the chest, on the floor, there was just enough room for me to curl up until it was safe to go back out again. Some nights we stayed in that closet until morning.

Looking back, it's hard to say how things proceeded as long as they did. In retrospect, I can see that even though we didn't mean to, my mother, my sister, my brothers, and I helped keep my dad going. My mother would make excuses for him, cover up, clean up the evidence of his violence. She dragged him to bed and told lies to protect the reality of our life. Sometimes my mother went to church with a black eye. If someone asked her how she got it, she would say, "Oh, I slipped and hit my head on the bathtub."

And I would think, "No, you didn't. Daddy hit you."

Over time, I got the message; some lies were okay. Putting on a happy face and acting as if everything were okay was the first big lie. No matter what happened the night before, I would go to

school and act as if everything were perfect. Lies to disguise anything unpleasant were acceptable. I might have been hearing it was
a sin to lie no matter what from the nuns at school and in the
Baltimore Catechism, but I was learning how to tell little necessary
lies at home. Faced with the awful reality of my dad's chronic
drinking, it's no wonder my mom avoided telling the truth, even to
herself. It's a truth I avoided for years until I finally decided to face
my past honestly, through writing *Keeping Secrets*. But there was a
long time in between when lying became one of my bigger problems.

My early lies were like my mother's. When friends from school
wanted to come over to the house, I said they couldn't. I told them
my father had just had an operation and was recovering at home.
Other times I made up all kinds of illnesses for him; anything to
keep those kids away. Because of this, I became isolated. I didn't
want to make friends because they might learn the truth.

Our day-to-day lives got crazier as time went on. Yet, we continued to pretend that nothing was wrong. I've kept a picture on
my dresser for many years. Recently I looked at it and realized
something that I hadn't appreciated for a long, long time. I remember what happened that night before that photograph was taken.
When my dad was drunk, he developed an obsession about left-
overs in the refrigerator. I don't know what triggered his anger, but
he couldn't tolerate seeing leftover food. He'd start tossing everything out of the refrigerator. Glass would break. The night before
that picture of me was taken, his tantrum had carried over to the
living room. He'd thrown the furniture and given my mother a
black eye. To look at me in that photo, you'd think I was the
happiest little girl in the world. Yet, only hours before I'd been
cringing upstairs, hoping the worst wouldn't come. It always did.
Always.

To me, that photograph sums up everything about my childhood.
Through whatever chaos and catastrophe my dad was causing, I'd
put on that happy face, the face I'd learned from watching my
mother. I'd deny the truth until I believed that denial myself. My
dad didn't even have to work at it. More often than not, on the
mornings after his worst tantrums he wouldn't remember a single

thing about his rampage. He'd been in a total blackout the whole time. All he knew was he felt terrible. He'd have the shakes and a terrific hangover. We'd walk on eggshells hoping not to do anything that would make him want to drink that night. As if we had any control over his drinking. We thought if we didn't upset him he might want to drink less or maybe not at all.

My sister left the house and got married at nineteen. Or should I say, my sister got married at nineteen to leave the house. Dan joined the Navy when he turned eighteen. After that, it was only myself and my little brother. I was fourteen years old and just starting to develop. For some reason, this sent my father into a rage. He was angry with me all the time. Incest was never an issue, but he'd come into my room and sit on the edge of my bed and tell me about sex in the most gruesome, awful way. If I walked around the house in my nightgown, he'd yell at me to put some clothes on. Before long, I was ashamed of my body.

Right around this time my mother made me a beautiful dress. It was for a dance that was to be held at school. I couldn't wait to wear it. At night I'd lie awake in bed wondering how I would look in it when that special night came. One night around three o'clock in the morning, I was trying to block out my dad's ranting and raving in the room next door. I kept praying he wouldn't come in and bother me. But, all of a sudden, the door to my room came bursting open, banging against the wall. I sat bolt upright. He came toward me. I thought, "God, he's going to kill me." The veins on his neck were bulging and he looked like he was frothing at the mouth. "You worthless, hopeless, useless tramp. You're a whore," he yelled. "You're gonna get knocked up!" I didn't even know what "knocked up" meant.

Instead of coming for me, he went right for my closet. "You think you're something special," he snarled. "You think your mother's making you pretty dresses so you can go out with the boys. Well, you're nothing!" He took my beautiful new dress and ripped it in half.

"No!" I screamed. "Daddy, please don't!" But he wouldn't stop. Then he reached into my closet for more clothes.

My mother came in screaming, "Are you crazy?" She tried to

grab the clothes from him, but he pushed her down and hit her in the breast. He really hurt her. I loved my mother; I couldn't stand to see him hurt her this way. She started crying. My brother Dan was no longer there to protect us. I felt crazed. I looked down; there was my tennis racket. Without thinking, I picked it up and lifted it over my head. Then, with all my might, I brought it crashing down on my father. I heard wood connect with flesh. Blood spurted out of his head like a geyser. He made a guttural sound, groaned, then fell to the floor.

"Oh, my God!" I screamed. "I killed Daddy. I didn't mean to kill Daddy." My mother told me to call the hospital. As I dialed she dragged him down the hall, through the living room, and out onto the front porch. She pulled him down the stairs, across the lawn, and somehow managed to get him into the car. I ran out of the house after her, screaming, "I'm sorry, Mommy. I didn't mean to kill Daddy." My mother was in such shock she couldn't even look at me. She just backed the car out of the garage and sped away. I took this as evidence that I was the terrible person my father had always told me I was. I fell to the ground sobbing.

I guess I was in a stupor, crying on the ground. After a while, I began to get my wits about me. I saw that I was covered in blood. Blood was everywhere: all over the porch, in the house, everywhere my mother had dragged my dad. All I could think to do was get rid of it. I don't think I was trying to cover up; I was just trying to erase the entire incident. I grabbed the garden hose and washed down the entire front porch. Inside I filled a bucket with soapy water and scrubbed the rugs in my room. Finally, around 5:30 A.M., all the blood was gone. I took off my nightgown and soaped down. Afterward, I sat huddled on the floor of my closet praying for God to let my father live.

As the sun was coming up, I heard our car pull into the driveway. From the window, I saw my mother walking my dad up the path. It turned out I'd given him a concussion and he'd had to have a lot of stitches. After that, my father and I were like caged animals. I was constantly on guard and he was always watching me.

In retrospect, I realize my clobbering him that way was really the first time any one of us had stood up to him to say that his behavior was unacceptable. But, at the time, I only felt guilty about having hit him. The minute I started cleaning up that blood I reverted back to our old ways: cover up, deny, get rid of the evidence. The sad thing was that none of us ever said, "Enough is enough," in a meaningful way. Because of that, we enabled Dad to keep acting out as a result of his drinking. The ramifications were predictable.

At age seventeen, I got "knocked up" exactly as my father said I would. Since I had such low self-esteem, I sought approval wherever I could get it. I loved my dad and I know he loved me, but he did not know how to express that love. I continued to seek his approval any way I could. The guy I wound up marrying—the father of my child—was the only guy my father ever liked. They drank beer together; they talked sports. So before I had a chance to know how *I* felt, I got pregnant.

I really believe God sent me my baby to keep me alive. At seventeen, I did not want to be pregnant. I did not want to have a baby. But the instant they pulled him from my body, I loved him. It was the purest feeling I've ever felt. They say babies can't see, but I swear my son could. Immediately after his birth, they held him in front of me and we made eye contact. He had such a worried look on his face, like, "You're my mother?" His stare was so potent that I blurted out, "I promise, I'm going to make a good life for you. I promise."

This guy I'd married didn't know what he was getting into. We started out having a very normal life together. We could get through an entire dinner without lamb chops flying across the room. We could sleep through a whole night without somebody's head getting bashed in. And instead of being grateful, I was bored! I'd lived my whole life not knowing if I'd make it through the night. I wasn't able to go from that kind of excitement, horrible though it was, to this normalcy. All those nights huddling with my family whimpering, "I hate Daddy," had left me crisis-oriented. I needed someone to manage, someone to lie for, someone to take care of. I required it to feel alive. I had numbed all my feelings to the degree that I felt nothing. Not sadness, joy, pain, or happiness. The only time I felt anything was when there was a crisis. My poor husband. He just wanted to make a nice life for us and for our baby, but he couldn't; I was too sick.

I ruined that marriage. When no crisis appeared, I created one. I had an affair with my forty-seven-year-old drama teacher—a man old enough to be my father. Like my dad, the guy was an alcoholic. Talk about gravitating toward the familiar! Not that I recognized this teacher's alcoholism at the time. He behaved differently than my father did. He didn't get violent; he was in some kind of subtle stupor most of the time. But since he was drunk, I found I could handle him better. I didn't know how to be with someone who was sober; I understood drunks. I could adapt to his moods. Anticipate them. He could become the focus of my life. So after only two years of marriage, I got a divorce. I was the first person in my entire family to be divorced. I was the first person in my small town. I had gotten "knocked up." Every bad thing my dad had ever prophesied about me seemed to be coming true. I was exactly what he'd always said I was: a big zero.

Ironically, at the same time, my sister, Maureen, and my brother Dan were beginning to drink alcoholically. You'd think after everything they'd witnessed as children, they'd never touch alcohol. Just as you might have thought the last thing I would have done was fulfill my dad's awful prediction by getting pregnant. But that's the insidiousness of this disease. No matter your best resolutions to the contrary, if you have the disease of alcoholism and start drinking, you're likely to start drinking alcoholically or find some way to distract you from the pain. At the time, I prided myself on the fact that I wasn't a drinker. Therefore, I must be okay. But I was living with the consequences of growing up the child of an alcoholic as surely as Dan and Maureen were.

To tell you the truth, I don't know why I didn't resort to booze. Maureen said the first night she got drunk was the first time she ever felt good about herself. God knows, I would have done anything to feel that way. But for whatever reasons, I just didn't look to booze. I don't know if I'm not an alcoholic or if the disease is just patiently lying in wait. I do know that to this day I'm vigilant about the substance. I can't afford not to be.

Back then I chose other methods of trying to boost my sense of self-worth and push my pain away. I spent money I didn't have. It was as if, if I could dress well enough, I might begin to think I was good enough. I was barely making a living as a model, making between $3,000 and $5,000 a year. I didn't know what else I could do. I didn't feel prepared for anything. So I'd get occasional modeling jobs, but never very glamorous assignments. I was too short, too busty, and I didn't have the cheekbones for it. They usually made me the mother with the soap box or the girl next to the Chevrolet. Some months I would earn enough to get the rent together—which at the time was $200—but something would come over me and I'd find myself driving to the store. Next thing I knew, I'd spent everything I'd earned in a spree. I'd spent the rent money and then some. If there wasn't a genuine crisis, I would create one. I now realize that I did because I required crisis. It was familiar. Every night of my childhood had been a crisis and now I couldn't live without it.

During this time, I met the man I eventually married and am married to today. He was the host of a television show called the "Anniversary Game" and I was hired as a prize model. I walked into the studio that first day and, as they say in the comic books, "Boing!" There was an immediate chemistry. He asked me out and I was surprised; I didn't think a man like him would want to go out with somebody like me.

I fell in love with him immediately. On our first date, he started asking me about myself and my family. "What does your dad do?" he asked. I didn't want to be the daughter of the town drunk anymore, so before I knew what I was doing, I told him my dad was dead.

We started dating quite a bit and my lies kept coming. I told him my father had been a doctor—another lie. I couldn't introduce him to my mother, because she would blow my whole story. So I told him she was traveling around the world on her inheritance. For good measure I threw in that I was living off my inheritance. That's why I was living so well. I was one sick cookie. This whole time I was renting apartments I couldn't afford and charging up clothes and furniture I couldn't afford either. Crisis, crisis, crisis. Two years went by and we continued to see each other. During this entire time I lied about my past.

One Christmas I was in the kitchen making a soufflé. As I was whipping the egg whites, Alan walked in holding a Christmas

card. Something was wrong; I could tell by the look on his face.
"What's this?" he asked.

I thought, "Oh no, I'm caught." But I made a feeble attempt at
continuing the deception anyway. "Well, ever since Dad died,
Mom's really been crazy. She can't deal with it, so she signs all her
cards, 'Love, Mom and Dad.' "

Alan just looked at me for a long time. Finally he said, "You're
all messed up, aren't you?"

I couldn't speak. I wanted so much to keep lying. Instead I
answered him honestly. "Yeah," I said, "I'm all messed up. Every
single thing I've told you since the day I met you is a lie, except that
I love you. That's the only honest thing."

We stayed up all night and I told him everything. I told him that
my father was the town drunk. I told him that my mother was being
thoroughly beaten down by his disease. Her hands and hairline
were laced with psoriasis caused by stress. Her hands shook. She
couldn't make eye contact with anyone. My elder sister and
brother were getting drunk every night. My younger brother was
an alcoholic and drug addict and had stopped talking at age
twelve—just stopped talking. I told him that I had been to my
parents' house two days earlier and that when I walked through
the back door, my father didn't even know who I was. He was that
drunk.

When I finally finished, Alan said tenderly, "This has hurt you a
lot more than it's hurt me. Let's start over with the truth now." He
said the stories I'd told him had never rung true. He said he loved
me, not the person I'd made up. I learned something very valuable
that night; I was lovable. If I really had to point to a watershed
moment in my life, that was it.

Shortly after Christmas, I was presented with a kind of crisis I
never would have sought. My little boy was riding a skateboard
he'd gotten for Christmas when he lost control and shot out into
the street, just as a car was coming over the hill. The car ran over
him, caught him by his little peacoat, and dragged him. From inside
the house I heard the crash. I immediately ran out, only to find him
lying in the middle of the cul-de-sac. The car was about fifteen feet
ahead of him. The driver's door was open but there was nobody

inside. My little boy was all alone and blood was running down the hill. I raced out and picked him up. His head was split wide open. He said, "Mommy." Then he passed out.

The doctor told me his chances of pulling through were fifty-fifty. His spleen had been crushed. I prayed that night to my God, the one that had been inside me, who understood me. Thankfully, my son survived. After he had spent many weeks in the hospital, I was at last able to bring him home. Both the lady who hit him and my ex-husband had very little insurance. I wound up owing $20,000. So now I was plagued by a new crisis: the constant calls and threats of a collection agency.

I always hate to hear it—it sounds so Polyannaish—but out of nearly every bad experience there can come some good. This horrible accident ended up leading me to one of the best things that ever happened to me and my son. After he came home from the hospital, he started having terrible nightmares. He'd wake up in a cold sweat screaming and sobbing. No amount of rocking him helped. I was beside myself. I didn't know what to do. When your child hurts, you hurt worse. In the end, I took him to the community mental health center. They charged me according to my ability to pay. One dollar per visit.

This wonderful woman, a social worker, began working with him. After a year of treatment, she said, "He's okay. He doesn't need to come any more. He doesn't have the nightmares or the fear. He's very well-adjusted. You've been a good mother."

That made me feel wonderful. I'd promised him I'd take care of him back in the delivery room and here was this nice woman—a professional—telling me I'd succeeded. But then she said, "I'd like you to stay. You have the lowest self-esteem of anyone I've ever met." I was startled, to say the least. I had never really given my self-esteem much thought until then. I didn't know it, but my life was about to change dramatically through this woman's aid.

"Make a list," she said. "On one side put down the good things about yourself and on the other, the bad." For a year, the good side never had a single thing on it. The bad side was filled with items spilling over to the other side of the page. But, in the end, after many visits, I started thinking of positive attributes to jot down.

"I have some talent," I told her one day.

"Really?"

"Yes," I said. "I used to get the leads in school plays and musicals. Not that I could do anything like that for a living."

"Why not?" she asked. "Why couldn't you? Have you thought about that?"

"I do a little modeling, but I don't get much work."

"Why not?"

"Because I'm not as good as the other . . ."

"Why not," she snapped back. "I think you have a lot to offer. I think it shows you're very talented, that you got leads in school plays. What else is good about you?" Little by little she helped me find the answers.

After three and a half years of therapy, I finally felt good enough about myself to say to Alan, "I want to be married. I've been with you for many years. What are your intentions for me? I can't go on like this."

This was very new for me—demanding that I be treated well. Before, I felt lucky for any affection or approval I got. But now I felt deserving of good things. Good things began to come my way. I got a Honda commercial, then one for Rice-A-Roni. I wrote poetry and got it published. Each of these achievements raised my self-esteem a notch. My therapist raised it. "You do have talent. You do have something to offer. You do have something to say."

Then I was booked on "The Tonight Show" because of my poetry. I remember walking out in front of the audience thinking, "How did I get here?" When I was chosen to appear as Chrissy on "Three's Company," I felt that way again. I feel very lucky, very fortunate for the life I'm leading today. But if it hadn't been for the years of therapy and that one therapist who caught me by accident at precisely the right time, I don't think I'd be in a position to enjoy good things that come to me. I'd still be the old me, thriving on chaos, creating crises when none exist, sabotaging every happiness.

These days I can hardly relate to my former self, the little girl who had the lowest self-esteem of anyone her therapist had ever met. Every now and then when I'm feeling down or insecure, I get a glimmer of her. Thankfully, I've left her behind. But before I could leave her, I had to own up to what really went on in my childhood. Only then could I see the motives behind my patterns of behavior. And only then could I begin to abandon those old patterns and ways of thinking entirely.

I'm not the only one in my family in recovery today. A day at a time—my dad hasn't had a drink in fifteen years. My brothers and sister are sober, too: Maureen for seventeen years, Dan for ten, and Michael for seven. My mother has been in the process of regaining her self-esteem through therapy and she is making incredible progress. Two decades ago I would not have thought these changes possible. Without self-help programs, I and the members of my family might have been doomed to live out lives carved by the disease of alcoholism . . . or die, as do so many alcoholics. Today, a new freedom is possible. It takes time. It takes work. As they say in twelve-step programs, it's an inside job; nobody can do it for you. But the rewards are deeper than I could ever calculate.

Today I say that I'm grateful to be the child of an alcoholic. (I'm more grateful still to be the adult child of a *recovering* alcoholic.) Through my own recovery, I've been granted a lease on my life I never would have had, had I not endured my particular childhood. I don't know that I could have come to this level of consciousness any other way.

*There are always suicides
among people who are unable
to say what they mean.*

JOHN IRVING

Dee Wallace Stone

DEE IS BEST KNOWN *as the mother in Steven Speilberg's movie, E.T., as Dudley Moore's sobbing one-night stand in 10, and as the mother on the syndicated series "Lassie." She has appeared in countless television shows and movies.*

Twenty years ago, Dee Wallace and I were both studying acting with Charles Conrad. Every time we were asked to do a scene, Dee would sob, no matter what the scene, comedy or drama. She would sit in a chair across from the other actor and tears would start rolling down her face. I could never figure out how she could summon those tears on command. At the time, I chalked it up to her ability as an actress. Indeed, her talents are considerable. But I now realize that Dee was tapping into a reservoir of pain that had been filling her since childhood.

Dee loved her father more than anyone in the world, but his alcoholism deprived her of his support. His suicide left her feeling empty and wondering what she might have done to help him. She felt great shame and guilt for failing to be enough for him. It's taken her a long time to shed that sense of responsibility.

Dee's story is an example of a little girl who wanted nothing more than her father's love and attention. But her father was only able to give her that love intermittently, between his frequent bouts with alcohol. As his drinking increased, Dee was squeezed out further still. But the perfect little girl put on the perfect little face to greet the world. From her appearance, no one could know anything was wrong. But inside, Dee was crushed to see the father she adored gradually desert her through the abuse of alcohol.

Dee has been happily married to Chris Stone for eighteen years. Three years ago, she had their first baby. Dee hopes to raise her child in the kind of home and family environment she would have wished for herself.

DEE WALLACE STONE

$\mathcal{M}$Y childhood was a constant teeter-totter, a constant yin and yang. When my father was not drinking, he was the best father in the world. I was his little angel. He could make me feel special, like nobody else in the world. But when he was drinking, he went from Dr. Jekyll to Mr. Hyde.

Luckily, there were very strong women in my family. My mother was well-respected and had enormous support in the community. I had very strong grandmothers who helped to raise me. So there was some stability. But my father, as much as I loved him, was always the wild card. From an early age, I felt a great deal of responsibility for my father and for my family. I did my best to keep my younger brother from seeing the worst of it. He was five or six when I was in high school. Every night I'd take him upstairs to bed before the fighting began. He'd come downstairs again and I'd always send him back up. In the end, I can't say I really spared him from anything, but it was very important to me that he be upstairs at the time.

I never saw my father hit my mother. It was all verbal abuse, but it was terrifying. And my father got very strange when he was drunk. Half the time he'd be running around the house nude. He became grossly overweight and swollen through his drinking, so he wasn't exactly a pleasant sight.

I'd do my best to protect my mother from his verbal assaults. There was so much fighting and screaming, and it would go on for hours. Nobody could sleep. Yet I felt it was up to me to control it. I really believed that our chance for happiness together as a family rested with me. I thought that my father could stop drinking if only he loved me enough. When he just couldn't quit, I blamed myself. I wasn't a good enough daughter. I felt like a failure. To compensate, I set out to be perfect in every other area in my life. No matter how much I succeeded, however, I still felt like a failure inside. I just wasn't able to be enough so that I could help him.

I don't know why I felt so responsible. My mother didn't depend on me for anything other than going to the front door to tell the bill collectors that no one was home, or going to the phone to tell my father's boss that he was sick.

We were always trying to cover up for him. We thought it was the only way. I remember one time when my father had been out of work for a very long time and a prospective employer called him early in the morning; Dad was so drunk we couldn't get him out of bed. My older brother was home from college at the time. Together we got Dad up and into an ice-cold shower just so he could talk to this person.

This kind of scenario was a way of life around our house, yet, if you asked me if I loved my father, I would say I loved him with everything in me—for all those ice creams, Christmases, and hugs.

My mother and grandmother tried to compensate for my dad's lack. They tried to fill the void he couldn't. Luckily, I could talk about things with my boyfriend and with my friends at church. Everybody in church knew about my father. It's hard to keep quiet that your dad's been a drunk for the last ten years. And besides, that's what church is for—support. Also, I would never have gotten through those years if it hadn't been for a wonderful couple, Bill and Donna Robinson, who were my counselors at the church. Sometimes they would come over and take me out of the house when it got too bad and I couldn't take it any more. Without ever putting my father down, they really helped me through. And they were always there to listen.

My dad got worse as the years went on. When I was in high school, he was really well into his disease. I have a lot of painful memories of this time. When I was up for homecoming queen, I went to him and said, "Daddy, I really want you to escort me, but only if you can promise me that you'll be sober."

He said, "Let me tell you tomorrow." Tomorrow came and with tears in his eyes he said, "I can't promise you." I know he wanted to but he just couldn't do it. So, one of my teachers escorted me instead. Many years later, my mother told me that Dad was up in the stands.

My dad did try to stop drinking, but he never had any luck. He'd gone to AA three or four times by then. He'd been in an alcoholic hospital. He just couldn't kick it. It was a sickness and it infected me. I had all his anger, frustration, and hurt inside me, but I didn't know why back then.

After a point, he was so beaten down and so drunk most of the time that he tried to kill himself—two or three times—usually in my bed. He slit his wrists a couple of times in my bed. We never discussed it. And even though he had tried so many times, I never thought he would actually do it.

The last time I ever saw my father was on Christmas my senior year of high school. My mother had finally split with him a few months before. He was living in another house. Christmas had always been really important to my dad; he was really into the holidays and making everything special. We never had a lot of money, but he always managed somehow to go down to this discount place on Christmas Eve really late to pick up everything they had. So he was awfully broken up about not living with us at this time.

My mother took us to see him that Christmas. He tried to make it special, but the only thing he had for us were some old coins. I think that did it. I think he was so upset that it pushed him over the edge. I never saw or spoke to him again. Three weeks later, he drove himself down to his favorite bar, parked behind it, and shot himself in the neck. The authorities found him the next morning.

My uncle came down to my high school to get me. I was called into the principal's office. I walked in and found him sitting there. He said, "There's been some trouble and you need to come home."

We headed for the car and I said, "Dad's dead, isn't he?" Kids have an uncanny way of knowing these things.

My uncle said, "Well, yeah, there's been an accident." I couldn't get much more out of him. By the time we got home my mother was sedated. I picked up little bits of what had happened here and there; I don't think anybody ever told me that he shot himself until my older brother came home.

I was the one who told my younger brother. I remember that more vividly than anything else about the whole incident. He was about eight years old at the time. A couple of his classmates had already come by and said something about it; he didn't know what they were talking about. Kids can be so cruel. I took him upstairs and told him what had happened. I remember his telling me, "You're a liar. Dad didn't do that. I hate you." So even beyond the end, there was such a strong urge for denial.

The next morning, a Friday, I insisted on going back to school. I was head cheerleader and there was a game that afternoon. When I got to school there were maybe four hundred kids gathered in the social hall for the pep rally. When I walked in, the whole place stopped. You could hear a pin drop. I walked in, took my place in line and called out a cheer.

Throughout the day, everyone—especially my teachers—would come up to me and say, "Gee, I think you're really brave to be here today." Looking back, I think I was just trying to be the perfect little girl who could stand anything.

When I think about my father's death now, it doesn't affect me as much as his life, because I feel like I watched him kill himself long before he committed suicide. I don't think I'll ever get over the sense of loss, but I feel I'm finally rid of that feeling that it was my fault, that I could have done something to change everything if he had just lived a little longer. I now know there was nothing I could have done.

When you're the child of an alcoholic, I think you grow up with this false sense of control and responsibility. You feel you're the only one who has to make him happy, you're the one who is supposed to call the doctor, you're the one who has to lie to the boss and the bill collector. I know I've carried that urge to control into my adulthood, both in my professional life and my personal life. I've really got to watch it.

My husband and I have been blessed with our beautiful three-year-old daughter. In parenthood, I'm rediscovering all the issues I thought I'd resolved in therapy years ago. The old wounds are open again. When she goes to Christopher and says, "Daddy, you want to come and play?" and Chris says, "No, honey, I'm watching the game," I think, "Please don't say that to her. How can you not make time for your own daughter?" I now realize it's my old issues coming up. I can understand that intellectually, but I still feel the pain in my gut.

I want to make everything all right for her. I want to be the "perfect mother," just as I tried to be the perfect daughter once. But to be that kind of perfect, I'd have to lose myself entirely. And it still wouldn't guarantee my daughter's happiness. To me, it boils down to a question of control. I just don't have the power, so I have to learn to let go and ease up.

I'd like to say to anyone reading this, if you think you're not leading the happiest, most fulfilling life you can lead, go get help. Whatever is troubling you, there are meetings for it, there are organizations across the country. If you don't want to seek a therapist, try a minister or a counselor. Anyone for a start. You owe it to yourself.

Women have to learn that
nobody gives you power.
You just take it.

ROSEANNE ARNOLD

Angie Dickinson

FROM BEAUTY CONTEST winner to starlet and finally to full-fledged movie star in films like Rio Bravo, Ocean's Eleven, *and Brian De Palma's* Dressed to Kill, *Angie captured the hearts of the American public. But she is best remembered as the star of television's long-running "Police Woman" series.*

Angie's childhood was full of tension and sadness. Her father's alcoholism dominated the household. She tried to stay out of his way, trying not to stir up trouble. Her mother was distracted—working and trying to provide as stable a home life as possible, while sustaining both physical and verbal abuse from a husband who seemed to despise her.

As a result, Angie didn't get much attention. She learned to cope, as children do, by fantasizing and creating a safe world within her own mind. Innately, she knew she had to take care of herself; and that is what she has continued to do throughout her life.

In between the glamour and the spotlights, Angie has dealt with her share of personal tragedy: the demise of her storybook marriage, a daughter born with severe eye problems, a sister completely debilitated by Alzheimer's disease, and the death of her father due to alcoholism.

ANGIE DICKINSON

I grew up in a small town in North Dakota during the Depression. For activity, the adults played cards, drank beer, and I guess made love. You know, those long, cold winter nights . . .

My father was never sober. He drank every day. He was abusive toward my mother. I'd see him slap her around, push her, knock her down. He'd call her stupid and a bitch. It was frightening to watch. I would beg him not to hurt her, and I would cry. Then I'd be spanked for crying. After a while, I learned not to cry.

To this day, I think of my childhood as a happy one, even though almost all of my memories of my father are of him drunk. We just accepted his drinking. It was such a constant, a fact of life. I didn't wonder about my father's drinking any more than I wondered about the color of his hair; it was just the way it was.

I think part of the reason I didn't see my life for what it was lies in my Libra nature. My head is just naturally up in the clouds. That's my way of avoiding unpleasant realities. It's as if subconsciously I think, "If I don't acknowledge it, it doesn't exist." I think this is the way I've been able to persuade myself that my childhood was truly happy. Avoidance like this can work for a while, but only up to a point, as I found out later in life.

I've heard other children of alcoholics refer to "the secret," but my father's drinking was never anything secret in our small town. The population was seven hundred but the people were so spread out, it felt more like fifty. I don't think there was anyone who didn't know my father as the town drunk.

Maybe it wasn't a secret, either in our family or around town, but a lot went unsaid. No one in my family ever openly referred to my father's drinking. My mother never talked about the beatings. See, we were not only an alcoholic family, we were a German alcoholic family. Between the cultural tradition, the disease, and that time period, there wasn't a lot of enlightened thinking about how to discuss the kind of problems my father's drinking caused.

There were some terrible moments, but it was like a broken romance; you get used to the pain after a while until you don't notice. I think that's how I finally convinced myself that mine was a happy childhood. Don't get me wrong, in a lot of ways it was happy. But through the influence of my father's drinking, my parents' marriage was never a happy one. That hurt a lot. And my father was never the kind of nurturing parent you'd hope to have. He was just too drunk.

I never hated my father, but I hated the way he behaved. When he was drunk, he would curse endlessly. It was like some awful kind of chant with "goddamn" as the central mantra. "Goddamn. That goddamn door. Get out of here, goddamn it. Get out of here." It was just an endless series of drunken complaints.

Looking back, I realize now that my mother was incredibly strong. I didn't think of her that way then, since she never stood up to my father. But she really held the family together through rough times. She accomplished the Herculean task of putting out the weekly paper that was our livelihood. Besides that, she ran the household. That meant cooking, cleaning, laundry, marketing, canning, gardening, washing, ironing, sewing, preparing meals, and managing my father.

Between my mother's quiet strength and my father's congenital weakness, I didn't grow up expecting to rely on a man. I never had as a child, because my mother never did. So that was one wonderful gift I had from childhood, and one I never appreciated until later in life. I always fully expected that the only person I could truly rely on was myself. I realized very early I would have to earn my own living if I ever hoped to have any peace or any control in my life.

When my first important relationship with a man began to develop, I handled it very poorly. I certainly had little to go on; my parents hadn't been able to set much of an example of what a loving, mutually nurturing relationship should be. So I married the wrong, although lovely, young man. He was very sweet. He just had the misfortune of meeting me at a time when I was just beginning to understand myself. I really wasn't prepared to be a partner to another person.

I was so restless in that relationship, I sought other diversions. Eventually, I entered a beauty contest, which started my career. I never thought of myself as being beautiful, but I guess I thought, "Why not? Maybe I'll get lucky and the judges will be cross-eyed." I entered and won and that sparked my interest in acting. At first it was just an escape, but it really paid off.

When I left my first husband, it was very painful. I pursued acting more vigorously after we split up, but I never thought, "I'm going to make it to the top in acting." I just had the desire to be free and get a job. Of course, I wanted to get a better job with each job that I got. I also wanted to be accepted. As a kid, I'd always worked hard in school to get A's just so I wouldn't embarrass myself. I could never control my father enough to prevent the embarrassment of having him show up drunk, but I could control me. From a very early age, I determined never to do anything that might humiliate me.

Ten years after my first marriage, I married Burt Bacharach. We had a daughter together. I didn't know it at the time, but looking back I realize I had a tendency to be very controlling. I wanted to be in charge, yet I always did what Burt wanted me to do. In our home I felt I was in charge, but I always asked him what he wanted for dinner. I was like a manager. I wanted to control things so my husband and child would be happy. I guess I'm a lot like my mother that way.

I consider myself very spiritual today. I think that's why I'm not a spoiled person. I'm not materialistic. I believe in a very powerful force and being connected to it. When I was really graduating into life, my one very important guru said, "There is only one mind." That's stuck with me, and the more it registered the more powerful a statement I realized it was. It is hard to explain, but I guess it's

71

a little like belief in God; if you believe, no explanation is necessary; if you don't, no explanation is possible.

Nowadays, I spend a lot of time thinking about how I really feel about things. Instead of just going through life thinking I'm happy, which worked for a while, I'm learning to be happy with reality. It is important to face who you are, and what you are, and what you want. Therapy helped me get my head out of the clouds and look at my life for what it was. I used to think therapy was some narrow library of a room where you lay on a couch and bored a doctor with your life story. But now I think there's a lot to be said for the kind of perspective therapy can bring. I think it would be wonderful if everyone would consider it. I think our schools should teach music, parenting, and marriage skills—skills that could contribute to the happiness of individuals and, in consequence, society.

I've forgiven my father's disease for depriving me of knowing who he was. I have nothing but love and understanding for him today. I only wish I could have had a better understanding of alcoholism as a disease a little earlier.

In the last couple of years of his life, I found my father on Skid Row in such bad shape that I took him home with me. At the time, I just had a little place of my own; I couldn't keep him there for long. I didn't think I could dip into my savings to support him and I couldn't know I would continue to do well. But I still feel guilty—for not being more of a parent to my father, I guess. I wish I had put him up in a little apartment so I could check up on him and make sure he had enough to eat. But I didn't.

To this day, I feel sure that had I been more loving and generous, I could have stopped his drinking. But I know that's just my ego talking. That's the old me still trying to control. I can't help it. I still wish I could take care of my father today. And I'm more determined than ever to take care of my sister, Mary Lou, who now has Alzheimer's.

If someone reading this relates to the little girl I used to be or has difficulty acknowledging her feelings as I did, I would say, "The head-in-the-clouds works for a while, but then you have to find the wisdom to know when to face reality."

*If you don't forgive
yourself, you cannot grow and will
never get beyond the anger.*

Patti Davis

THE LAST THING *Patti Davis ever hoped to be was First Daughter. But when Ronald Reagan's political aspirations led him from his post as California's governor to the presidency of the United States, she found herself in the unwanted role.*

As early as a decade before her father's ascension to the presidency, Patti had sought to avoid being swept up by his political prominence by legally changing her surname from Reagan to Davis, her mother's maiden name. She never wanted to cash in on the Reagan name, particularly since her own political views are at such odds with her father's.

According to Patti, Nancy Reagan never approved of anything she—Nancy's only daughter—ever did. So why would Patti choose her mother's maiden name as her own? Possibly it is the only way she can feel any link to her. To this day, it remains their only true connection.

The most striking aspect of Patti's modest home in Santa Monica is the fact that there is absolutely no clue—no memorabilia or photographs—that indicates her father spent eight years of the 80s in the White House.

After some stabs at acting, Patti turned her talents to the endeavor that had long been her only solace growing up: writing. Her first novel, Home Front, *was a* New York Times *best seller. She has completed two other novels, and her autobiography,* The Way I See It, *was published this past spring.*

Patti shares her home with Sadie, a dog she rescued from the pound, and Squirmy, a pet squirrel abandoned by its mother.

PATTI DAVIS

I'M a victim of alcoholism two generations removed. It is still playing a role in my family's life, even without the actual alcoholic being there. My father is the child of an alcoholic. His father's drinking made him extremely erratic and emotionally unavailable for my father. As a consequence, my father was not emotionally available to me. He didn't know how to nurture me or get close.

There's a story about my father sitting in the Oval Office. There was a fire in the next room, but he stayed where he was. He didn't refuse to leave; he just didn't react. My father learned not to feel because feeling was too painful. He pretended that things were better than they were. He couldn't depend on the most important person in his life, so he learned not to trust. He learned to survive in a crazy, alcoholic environment. When his father was acting crazy, my father would just go into his room and sleep. His way of dealing with the stress was not to deal with it at all.

Some might argue that I don't have any right to complain. My parents didn't torture me. I wasn't sexually abused. What abuse I suffered was of the passive sort. I was emotionally abandoned from day one. Looking back, I don't think my parents were at all malicious in the way they neglected me. I just think they are the sort of people who never should have had children. My mother means all the world to my father. She, in turn, adores him. I've never really witnessed anything like it. There just wasn't a place for the children. No void for us to fill, no desire. From as early as I can remember, I felt isolated, frightened, and insecure.

I didn't have many close friends in school. My parents told me that when they picked me up from school, all the other kids would be playing on the playground, but I'd be sitting off by myself under a tree reading a book.

It was easier for me to stay by myself. My solitude was something I could hang on to. I was fine by myself. Anything, so long as I wasn't under other people's scrutiny. I was so sure I'd never measure up. I think my solitude and the solace I found in reading is what led me to write.

My mother and I were at odds with each other. She never seemed pleased about anything I did. I wasn't the sort of daughter she expected. I didn't look the way I was supposed to look. I didn't dress the way she thought I should. And she was always this impeccably dressed fashion plate. As a child I always wanted her approval; but I just couldn't or wouldn't go to her lengths to get it. It took me a long time—until I was in my thirties—before I realized my parents would never accept me. We simply don't get along. But I don't resent them for it.

As a child, I tried to get close to my father, but there's something very distant and intangible about him. He's such an enigmatic man. He's fun to be with, but you don't really get a sense of who he is. You can only go so far. My mother penetrated the shield that separates him from other people, but I could never make any closer contact than I would have if I'd been a waiter or a guy pumping gas. I mean, my father's nice and congenial to everybody. He's a nice man. I got that same nice man. I didn't get anything special. I never got to know him any better than a waiter would.

That's one thing about my father. You may disagree with his politics, but he's completely sincere. What bothers me about him politically is that his well-crafted vision of things is not found in reality. It's a lot of *Reader's Digest* slogans. It sounds good, but scratch the surface, and you ask yourself, "Where is this coming from? Is this really the way it is?"

My father's vision of the world is black and white. For him, good and evil are as clear-cut in life as they are in a John Wayne movie. I don't think the world is that simple, but I'm very aware of how seductive his vision was. I understand why he was elected. People want to hear that everything is fine. His view of childhood was crafted the same way. He wanted everything to be wonderful, so it was.

I've never discussed my father with my half-sister, Maureen. My family is like a fleet of separate ships; nobody talks to anybody else. But I got some insight when Maureen was on "Donahue" promoting her book. When she told Phil that she had left her abusive husband and moved to the YWCA, he said, "What do you mean? Jane Wyman is your mother, Ronald Reagan is your father. Why didn't you go home? Why'd you move into the YWCA?"

Maureen took a deep breath and said, "When I was seven years old and got sent away to school, I decided I was never going to rely on anyone ever again; that my life was mine to take care of. And I was never going to turn to anyone else to take care of it."

Listening to that I thought, "Whoa, that's exactly how I felt."

I still can't look at pictures of myself as a child. When we were moving from one house to another, I threw away two or three huge scrapbooks that my mother gave me. I had this box full of my childhood photos and I said to my husband, "You know, I'm going to go out to the trash and throw all this stuff away. I'm going to throw away my childhood." And I did. In every picture I had this frightened, pained expression on my face, like a frightened deer.

It was hard for me to look at myself then, and it still is today. But I'm not going to pull my father's trick and con myself into thinking everything was rosy, even though that is what I learned growing up. Once I realized that my sense of self-esteem was not going to come through my parents, I had to build it on my own. Every bit of confidence I have, I built on my own.

It wasn't easy. For a long time I had fantasies about getting closer to my father, about finally breaking through that wall of his the way my mother did. I've often thought it might be different if I'd been a boy. I think my mother resented having another woman around.

When I was older, I avoided speaking out politically because I knew my views wouldn't go over well with my parents. Then I decided to get involved in the anti-nuclear movement anyway. It was hard. My parents' friends called to tell me I'd "never work in this town again." Their agent friends called and said, "You know, people don't like it here when you get political." There was a negative cloud floating over my head.

Then I met Ron Kovic (the author of *Born on the Fourth of July*) at an anti-nuclear rally. He was a man on a mission. I looked at him and what he had to live with every day, yet he'd wheel himself out on that stage and raise a fist. I would think, "Man, if he can be doing this after what he's been through, then I can get through the obstacles in my life after all. What do I have to put up with? That my parents are disappointed in me? What else is new?" Seeing Ron put everything into perspective.

Pulling away from my family was the only way I saw of getting my life back. I'm happier now. I'm protecting myself. The less I see of my parents, the less frequently I entertain the futile hope of winning their love and approval. It's easier this way.

*Forgiving is a way of reaching out
from a bad past and heading out
to a more positive future.*

Desi Arnaz, Jr.

AT AGE FORTY, *Desi Arnaz, Jr. looks exactly like his father on the "I Love Lucy" show: yet there is a difference. It's in the eyes: the defensiveness of someone who's gone through a lot and doesn't have an easy time trusting new people. He has a sense of humor and a big booming laugh. Immediately apparent is his genuine love for Lucille Ball, Desi Arnaz, Sr., and his sister, Lucie Arnaz. But his story is sad in that it has taken so long to put behind him the years lost to alcohol and drug addiction coupled with angry parents, an alcoholic father, and a broken home.*

His parents' fame affected his life in every way. He constantly had to explain that he wasn't Little Ricky. He tried to be perfect, he tried to make things all right; but the job was beyond him. He became a serious little kid, a thinker who questioned everything. According to the press, his family had it all; yet his home life was living proof that money and fame don't bring happiness.

Desi's outlet was music. It was almost his demise: too much success, too soon, too fast. The press dubbed him undeserving—the rich son of famous parents who didn't have to work hard like the rest of us. But Desi has worked hard to get his life together. Fortunately, before the deaths of his parents, he was able to find resolution with them. Through his efforts, his unhappy past has been turned into his opportunity.

DESI ARNAZ, JR.

$\mathcal{T}$HE whole thing was an incredible cover-up. My parents happened to be two of the most important people on the planet, who were being told by millions that they were the perfect example of what a relationship should be. Everyone thought my parents knew what life was all about. If they were not happy, they had to pretend they were happy; and it weighed heavily on them. I couldn't tell anybody the truth. I had to keep it a secret. My whole life was keeping a big secret.

My room was right next door to my parents' room, so I heard everything. I was there the first time I heard them fight and I was shocked. They were yelling, screaming; it was bad. And it got worse over the years.

My father had a very, very, violent temper. Physical things happened. My mother wasn't a pushover, either, but she wasn't violent. She stewed for a long time, so you knew it was coming. But with Dad there was no warning. It would just erupt. That's what happens with alcohol; you just snap.

When I was very young I started learning about being defensive, hostile, negative, and aggressive. Drugs and alcohol lit a fire under that. At a very young age I developed my father's temper. That's how I handled my life. I'd yell at my friends. Not only that, I thought having a bad temper meant that I cared because what I learned by watching my parents was that this was how they cared. "Can't you see how much I care? Can't you see how much I love you? Can't you see how angry I am? That's because I care so much." I thought that jealousy meant that one person really loved the other person.

High-anxiety emotions—anger, jealousy, rage—all passed themselves off as a father who cared, who loved me. He didn't get angry because he was *wrong;* he got angry because he was *right.* He was so right he wanted to tell me how right he was, and the worst anger of all showed itself when he was sure he was right.

I can clearly remember when my parents got divorced. Their relationship had lasted twenty years. I loved them both and still do; but they weren't able to understand how to live their lives together. They weren't able to do what they needed to do in order to be happy. It was better for them to separate because they weren't helping each other at all, and somehow, innately, I knew that. I didn't think it was my fault. I just remember feeling relieved that now they would stop yelling at each other.

When I became successful with my band, "Dino, Desi, and Billy," I had a good perspective on it. But I was deceived by my own ignorance. I thought we could stay up all night, drink and use drugs, and not die; and I thought it would make me feel better. It didn't. It made me feel acutely ill.

I was never hit over the head with any real kind of real information about alcohol. In fact, I was shown people who were praised for this type of activity; highly successful people who were kind of charming when they were drinking. I didn't know anyone who wasn't drinking when I was growing up. By the time I was thirteen years old, this was the world in which I circulated. I was out performing with adults, and they all drank, so I drank too.

Nobody around me really knew I was using drugs. If they did, they didn't know the severity of it. In those days drugs didn't seem to be such a problem. I was out on the road in hotels when I was thirteen or fourteen and was self-sufficient financially. "Dino, Desi, and Billy" started making a lot of money, and it was like a flood my parents couldn't stop. Life was out of control; I was too young to have no boundaries. I had everything I could ever have hoped to have. All my dreams came true by the time I was a teenager. If there was something that would make me happy, I had the wherewithal to go after it. If I had a crush on someone famous, I'd just go meet her.

By eighteen, I had everything, but I was still looking for answers and getting none. Why do people have dreams? What is it that you're driven by? What's really important in this life? On the outside my career couldn't have been better, but I was slowly and surely getting in the way of myself because of drugs. I looked like I couldn't do anything wrong; but my life had become a re-creation of my childhood, because the person I was on the outside had nothing to do with who I was on the inside. I was physically ill for a long time. Because of marijuana, cocaine, and alcohol, nothing worked anymore.

I was killing myself. At this point I got treatment because somehow I realized the drugs weren't making me feel good anymore.

My sister was having her own ups and downs, not with drugs and alcohol, but with relationships that weren't working early on. We were close. She's a year and a half older than I am, and we never had bad times between us as most siblings do. We were able to talk. We found solace in one another. When frightening things happened in the house, I could go to her. When I went through recovery at a drug and alcohol treatment center, the strangest thing happened. I looked at her and we both started to cry. We weren't allowed the time to comfort one another in the house growing up. If we did that too much, our parents would ask, "What are you comforting each other for? What's there to be comforted about?" We would have to pretend, "It's not as bad as all that." We learned to minimize. My recovery was very emotional for my sister and me because she had a lot of unresolved, pent-up pain and fear, and we just started crying. I always loved my sister, but when I went through my recovery, we rediscovered each other.

Everyone in my family went through recovery with me—Mom, Gary Morton (her husband), Lucie, and my dad. It was important for all of them. Through recovery I learned I had to change my life completely. I had almost killed myself. I knew I could no longer live the way I had been living. It was life and death for me.

I finally found a way to understand everything that had happened, but not many people are interested in giving up the past. It's like being a newborn baby, pure and clean. I have a whole new thought process. I'm letting go of old ideas. It's a hard concept to take on. It doesn't mean you don't exist; it means you look at it in a different way.

If I had to label Desi Arnaz, Jr., at this time, I would say I'm a grateful student of Vernon Howard and the New Life Foundation. Vernon Howard is the author of many books on inner health and is the founder of New Life. Through them I have learned powerful spiritual principles that have changed me and saved my life.

I can remember as a child that this life didn't make much sense. Now I believe I've found the answers to my questions. They were inside me all the time, but I needed to go on an incredible journey to find them.

The reason to forgive is to regain your own emotional freedom and peace of mind.

Cindy Williams

THE FILM THAT WAS *Cindy Williams's first big break was also my first break into movies. In 1973, Cindy starred in the hit movie* American Graffiti. *I was cast as the mysterious blonde in the Thunderbird.*

I remember being somewhat awed by Cindy on the set. She was friendly and outgoing; I was intimidated by her because she had such a big part. (Remember, this is me twenty years ago, long before therapy helped me form a sense of self-esteem.) Cindy was at ease with the director, George Lucas, and playful with Richard Dreyfuss, another one of the stars.

Cindy subsequently enjoyed great success in the movie The Conversation, *in which she starred with Gene Hackman, and also with her hit comedy series, "Laverne and Shirley." When I landed the part of Chrissy in "Three's Company", it was my good fortune that our show followed the popular "Laverne and Shirley" every Tuesday night.*

As it turns out, Cindy and I have more in common than our old Tuesday-night time slots. Like me, Cindy was raised in a home warped by her father's alcoholism. Beneath that calm, confident exterior I'd so admired on the set of American Graffiti, *Cindy was nursing a lot of the same insecurities as I. Like me, she found salvation through therapy, which she sought after reading an article about alcoholism in* Newsweek. *She identified with every single behavior listed as those shared by adult children of alcoholics.*

Today Cindy, the mother of three children, continues to work as an actress in television and the movies. She and her husband, Bill

Hudson (of the Hudson Brothers) live in a gray clapboard house overlooking the ocean in Malibu, the kind of house from storybook watercolorings where the tale ends with "and they lived happily ever after."

CINDY WILLIAMS

I was afraid as a child and because of this fear I was extremely aware of everything, like peripheral vision, vision behind my head. I was even aware of whispers in the house. When I was a baby, my crib was located in my parents' room. We lived with my grandma in Texas. My crib had a decal at the foot of the bed with three little kittens dancing around a birthday cake. At night, the candles on the birthday cake would light up, music would play, and the three little kittens would join hands and dance. I felt they were angels watching over me, showing me beautiful, innocent things because something was going on. I can remember lying there pretending to be asleep but hearing sounds from my parents' bed—not sexual sounds, but scuffling noises. I know he was hitting her and I remember fear; but in my child's mind I hoped they were wrestling, like the people Grandma watched on television. There was always this gnawing feeling that something terrible was about to happen, like the sky was going to fall or something hideous was looming around the next corner; but I didn't know why. Looking back I can analyze it, but then it was just our way of life. That's how I saw the world and perceived everything. I've looked at pictures of myself as a child and I can see I'm never really smiling; it's like I'm always waiting for something to break loose.

I grew up in Irving, Texas. My mother worked as a waitress in Dallas, which was about ten minutes away. She worked a split shift, so she'd go to work in the morning, then come home in the early afternoon when I was at school. Then she'd leave again at two o'clock and wouldn't get back until 10 P.M. She always seemed to be leaving; that's when I started getting stomachaches. So from four-thirty to ten o'clock my younger sister, Carol, and I would be home with my dad.

He'd come around the corner in his truck and right away I could tell if he was drinking or not. I had an inner body clock. When it got past a certain time I'd hope for a miracle; maybe he wouldn't be drinking. If he was, I could tell by the way he hit the corner and by the time it took to get from the truck to the house because he had to hide his bottle.

Until I got married, four-thirty remained a bad time of day for me. It brought up all those frightening feelings of childhood when I was left in my father's care. It was really a time of anxiety and helplessness. How was Daddy going to act? Were we going to go out in the truck when he was drinking? If we did, he'd lock the doors and go inside the bar, leaving me in the truck. He'd buy me candy bars to keep me occupied and (I'm sure in his mind) happy. I can remember sitting in that truck watching the beer sign flash on and off while I was waiting for him: *Schlitz, Schlitz, Schlitz.* He had to get home before my mother did, because she'd flip out if she knew he was taking me to the bar. He'd say, "Don't tell." It was always to be our secret.

Sometimes he took me way out in the sticks to visit his aunt and her son, who was a spastic. My cousin and my dad would sit and drink while I sat in the kitchen watching the light bulb swing from a cord. My aunt would say, "I'll give you a cinnamon roll if you let me read to you from the Bible." I was scared out of my mind.

I was a scared little girl who was always waiting—waiting to get home, waiting in the car, trying not to fall asleep. I had to stay awake because he'd smoke and I'd have to check for cigarettes, because one night the chair caught on fire. It smoldered away until my mother came home and discovered it. I remember her screaming, "He's going to burn the house down." I felt like I was serving a master: a little caretaker, like a child in a Dickens novel. I was part of the conspiracy, part of the drunkenness, a sidekick in this sinister situation. As a child I accepted it because this was my dad.

I took on the same shame that I felt about him. I was ashamed of me.

When I was ten we moved from the country to a nice middle-class neighborhood in the Los Angeles suburbs. For a while I had a glimmer of hope that things might be different. But shortly after we arrived, my dad got drunk and beat the hell out of my new best friend's father. I remember lying in bed thinking, "Well, I can check off another door into hell. Now I know what it's like to experience this."

I remember scary rides home from the bar in my dad's truck. One night we got into an accident. My father had driven into a cement piling on the highway. He never saw it. His first concern was to be sure I was okay. For that instant, he sobered up. I wasn't okay, but I told him I was. I really hurt my leg and my knee was banged up. When we went home, he didn't tell my mother about it. That was another of our secrets.

Looking back, I can see how focused I was on my father. How was he feeling? Was he happy? If he was happy, I was happy. If he was upset, I was upset. It was a survival technique. I never learned to feel my own feelings or to develop normal reactions to situations.

As a child I developed a habit of taking a breath and holding it. I didn't realize I was doing it. I was just so anxious, so nervous all the time. There was always potential violence lurking in our household. I'd hold my breath, unknowingly, through every terrifying moment.

My father got worse as time went on. It got so anything could set him off. He could be really sweet, but then he'd change into this crazy, violent person. One night my grandmother gave us crosses for Easter. My dad was agnostic. He flew into a rage. The rest of the night he threatened to kill us all: first my grandmother, then my mother, then me. I was terrified. I really didn't know if he would do it or not. Alcohol made him so crazy.

My father never hit me or my sister, Carol, but he'd take me by the hair and thump me on the head. I could deal with that, but his verbal abuse was awful. I always wanted to be with my mother because I felt safer with her, so he started calling me "Momma's girl" in the most sarcastic, mean-spirited way. And then he would verbally abuse my mother to me. He gave so many graphic descriptions of the female gender. It was almost rendered meaningless, he did it so often. One of his many legacies is the fact that I cuss like a sailor. I can really go to town. Every New Year's Eve I have the same resolution: "I'm not going to curse." I start off the year with "heck" and "darn," but I'm always back to familiar vernacular by Valentine's Day.

I was a model child. I tried to be good so as to give him no reason to drink, but I couldn't find a way to please him. I now know it had nothing to do with me. But at the time I thought it was something I could control; I just felt so responsible.

The really tragic thing is, I can honestly say my dad was the smartest, funniest guy I've ever known. But when he drank, he wasn't funny. He certainly wasn't smart. When he drank, he was this other guy . . . the devil incarnate. At the same time, I knew he'd lay down his life to protect me, despite the precarious situations he often put me in.

Naturally, I wanted to be an emergency-room nurse; then I could take care of people in crisis situations. Taking care of my father the way I did, it's no surprise I wanted to make a career out of taking care of people. I knew I would have a great bedside manner, but I kept flunking physiology and a little voice kept telling me that physiology mattered a lot if you hoped to be an R.N.

Now I know that was just a screen, a way of avoiding my own feelings. Clearly, my father couldn't bear to feel, either. He had no sense of the good person that he was. I used to think that my father did what he did because I deserved such awfulness. Now I understand he had a disease, the disease of alcoholism.

I didn't grasp the ramifications his alcoholism held for me until I read an article in *Newsweek* that described the children of alcoholics. I fit the description to a T. For thirty years my life was haywire, then along came this article and I realized, "That's what I am and I better get help."

In my mind, I hadn't been important enough to have feelings. I had compassion for the entire world except for me. Now I've been able to get in touch with my feelings. I realize I'm not responsible for the whole world. And I'm not alone. God plays an important role in my life. When things get tough I can always turn to Him. I've got a family of my own that I love dearly and I'm working hard not to pass my old, warped view of the world on to my children.

I love my dad and have forgiven him for what his disease made him do to us. I've grown. I've begun to feel good about myself. That's the essence of my recovery. Of course there's one old habit I haven't been able to shuck . . . I still swear like a truck driver!

Physical Abuse

The worst scenarios of physical abuse are in the news almost every day: parents chaining their "uncontrollable" son in a closet for seventeen hours; a babysitter caught on home video slapping a child; a battered wife turning on her abuser. We are shocked when we hear about it. We gasp at the horror. Sometimes we even know their names. Who can forget the tragedy of six-year-old Lisa Steinberg, who died during one of the brutal beatings her adoptive father heaped on her?

Physical abuse has a face now and we can no longer pretend it doesn't happen in "nice" homes. You only have to read Gary Crosby's description of his father, Bing, using that famous golf swing of his to beat his sons until they bled to know that it can happen anywhere. And today, as alcoholism, divorce, and unemployment reach record-high numbers, people are less and less able to deal with the pressures. Wives get screamed at; kids get smacked; disgruntled employees attack their bosses; women get raped; minorities get bashed. But the wounds left by physical abuse are never just skin deep.

"Physical abuse does not exist by itself," explains Dr. Robert J. Ackerman, author of nine books concerning the effects of alcohol and abuse. "There's no such thing as physical abuse without emotional abuse. You can hit me. In all probability, I will recover from that; but why did you hit me?" As the victim of abuse searches for the answer to this question, untold emotional scarring occurs.

Randy Shilts's friends were puzzled by his deep depressions and severe migraines in high school. They didn't know that his mother was sadistically beating him almost every day. And long after the beatings stopped and the welts had healed, Randy's pain continued. He turned to drugs, alcohol, and eventually sleeping pills. "To me," Shilts said, "it is very clear that I got drunk to seek complete oblivion. I couldn't begin to live life without drugs or alcohol. As soon as I stopped using them, the pain started coming up—horrible memories and the feeling that everybody hated me in my childhood."

"In a physically abusive family," Dr. Ackerman continues, "one of the things kids learn unintentionally is that those who love you the most are most likely to hit you or yell at you or degrade you; and those are unintended consequences."

People whose lives are filled with this sort of domestic violence have a sense that there is no real meaning to their lives. They feel beaten down. Most of the time, they are unaware that options exist, that they can make other choices. They have feelings of guilt and shame and of not being as good as others, though they don't know why.

"I was always ashamed and I carried that shame with me my whole life," admits Sally Marr, victim of physical abuse and neglect and the mother of the comedian Lenny Bruce. "I wasn't sure what it was, but I just knew I didn't belong anywhere. I'd go next door and I'd see the mother washing her daughter's hair, brushing it, fixing it with bows and asking, 'Do you like this? Do you like that?' I knew I didn't have any of that."

Many of these survivors, like Judy Mitchell, subconsciously seek out the same type of abusive situations they knew as children, even though they believe it's the last thing they want. After life with an alcoholic father who beat her and her mother, who continually abandoned them, and who tried to dominate every aspect of their lives, Judy went through a string of controlling husbands and selfish boyfriends before turning into a hostile alcoholic—just like her dad. "Dad told me I was stupid. When *he* quit telling me, *I* told me I was stupid. I needed the negative reinforcement because I would not allow myself anything good."

"As adults, abused children tend to look for the same message they were sent in their childhoods," says Dr. William Rader, founder of the Rader Institute Eating Disorder Treatment Program. "A woman will marry a man who will beat her because she feels this is what she deserves. As a matter of fact, if he stops doing it for whatever reason, she'll divorce him and find another one." It is a learned behavior that fits with what she has been told. Judy Mitchell could never please her father; she thought she was a bad daughter. She wasn't able to please her husband, either. That fit with her already negative self-image and she was punished as she believed she should be. Under the influence of alcohol, she virtually mirrored her father's behavior, so it is not much of a stretch to imagine that he probably received the same type of treatment from his parents. And the cycle continues.

"Women carry shame more than men do. It's almost like it's their burden in life," says Carol Trenery, director of Sahuaro Vista Ranch, a women's treatment center in Arizona. "Women feel responsible, but they don't exactly know why. If she'd been a better mother, her son would not be in trouble. If she'd been a better wife, her husband would not have had an affair."

Brenda Clubine, a battered child who became a battered wife, agrees with that. "In between incidents, my husband would cry and tell me he was really sorry. He'd say it was stress or his mother, but mostly, it was me. If I wouldn't have said something in that tone of voice or if I would have done something I was supposed to, it wouldn't have happened. And, like when I was a little girl, I started to think it was me. My mother told me it was me; my second husband said it; my third husband said it. Everybody must be right. It's me."

Children will always blame themselves. "When I got beaten as a child," says Gary Crosby, "I thought it was because I was fat and ugly and didn't have any talent. I felt I couldn't do anything. I thought I deserved the abuse because I couldn't keep all of Dad's rules." Filled with rage at the injustice and severity of his punishment, Gary allowed that rage to consume him for years. Like so many others, he tried to stuff it down with food or numb it with pills and alcohol. But Gary's lucky; he stopped the cycle. Two of his brothers committed suicide.

It doesn't occur to a small child to question the adult, that the parent could be wrong. Adults are powerful figures in children's lives just by virtue of their position as a parent or important family figure. In addition to that, they're big.

Thomas Henderson was severely beaten by his mother. "I thought it was my fault. I'd go home and clean up the whole kitchen. I'd get diapers and hand-wash them. I'd sweep the yard. I only wanted to do good. It never made any difference."

As "Hollywood" Henderson, Thomas unleashed his anger on the football field. "I just wanted to go out there and beat the shit out of everybody. A lot of the characteristics of the way I played were the basic characteristics of the violence of my childhood."

"Many victims of abuse use anger for their own protection—as a shield to prevent anyone from getting close to them," says Della Hughes, Executive Director of the National Network of Runaway and Youth Services. "They are hurt and angry about what happened in their lives. They expect to be abused by all people in authority, be it teacher, police officer, or juvenile court worker. . . . Unfortunately, most of us fail to recognize the history that lies behind the anger and that the anger is serving a healthy purpose. Instead, we tend to further victimize these youths by punishing them for being rude and abrasive."

These feelings of confusion and anger are expressed in "Abused Child," a poem written by a seventeen-year-old girl:

> *My head is spinning with confusion.*
> *All I see are illusions*
> *Because of all the angriness that swims around me*
> *I feel no happiness.*
> *I feel as if I should cry but I can't*
> *Even though I try.*
> *I tried to talk to them and make them understand,*
> *But all I get is the backhand.*
> *Maybe someday they'll go up in the air.*
> *Why should I give a care?*

LISA MICHELL
Ukiah, California, from Sounds From the Streets:
A Collection of Poems, Stories and Art Work by Young People
© National Network of Runaway and Youth Services

Still other victims of physical abuse react in the opposite way, becoming nonconfrontational in their adult lives. "Often, they'll go to any lengths to avoid a confrontation, but the cost of being nonconfrontational is simply not to take care of yourself," Jerry Moe points out. "When you order in a restaurant and the dish you receive is not what you ordered, but you eat it anyway, that's not taking care of yourself. It can be as trivial as that; but if you can't assert yourself before a waiter you will never see again or a person who is rude to you on the phone, how are you going to do it with the people with whom you're intimate, when the stakes are much higher? When I see the nonconfrontational behavior, that's the child I'm most concerned about because that's a child who needs protection."

"Within a victim of abuse lurks a little child filled with confusion," says Dr. Rader. "That little child feels the outside world sees him as bad and wrong. Those feelings stem from a tragic, traumatic childhood. The abuse can have occurred once or it can have happened a hundred times; it has the same effect. Physical violence or just the threat of physical violence can traumatize that little child. The effects are difficult to reverse. That little child within becomes convinced that he is bad; the child has rationalized a justification for his beatings and that justification is the belief that he is bad and therefore deserving of punishment. I have to tell such people over and over, 'You are good. It's all right to let good things happen to you.'"

"It takes tremendous energy and strength to create negativity," Rader goes on. "People don't realize it, but to constantly be in the wrong place, to get in trouble, to come so close to what you want and then miss it means that you are doing a lot of intelligent work. When you come to the other side of wellness, you have all that intelligence and ability to move to the positive."

Jerry Moe believes children and adults can be taught healthy living skills that weren't present in their homes, "how to talk about feelings; how to be able to really share; how to find out that it's okay to be angry; that anger is an okay feeling and people can express it without yelling, without verbally or physically abusing— without putting you in jeopardy."

Ponder this: Adolf Hitler was an abused child; so was Saddam

Hussein. Later in life, they both acted out with unimaginable rage and insanity. In Gloria Steinem's new book, *Revolution from Within*, she points out that some of Hussein's supporters described him as brutal and harsh. In those rare instances where his childhood is described, the same words were used relative to his father. Yet, few have ever commented on this parallel. It seems so obvious. The behavior was learned and acted out in adult life.

"I feel very positive about the future," says Dr. Ackerman. "We are the first and largest group of adults who come from dysfunctional families who are acutely aware of our desire to be emotionally healthy. We're now trying to find the purpose to our lives because of our past. We have a whole generation of people who are not going to let dysfunction make them sick."

*Abusive parents are so
delusional in their thinking,
they come to believe they are
behaving this way in their
children's own best interest.*

Gary Crosby

I GREW UP ON Bing Crosby and Bob Hope's road movies. I watched the pair sing and dance their way through exotic locales like Rio, Morocco, and Singapore. Then there were Bing's fabulous Christmas specials. His children would sit at his feet looking up at him adoringly while he sang "Silent Night," "Joy to the World," and "Have Yourself a Merry Little Christmas."

Christmas was always the worst time of year in my own crazy, alcoholic home. I'd watch those Christmas extravaganzas wishing I could be as lucky as the Crosby kids. They seemed to have it all: a wonderful home, clothes, and money to buy anything life had to offer. But most of all, they had a fine, kind, loving father who was loved the world over. Bing Crosby was one of the most respected men of his time, a renowned good Catholic who regularly hobnobbed with the Pope and presidents of the United States. How I longed to be part of that kind of family. "Some people were just born lucky," I thought.

Knowing what I now know about Bing Crosby, I can't even listen to "White Christmas" anymore.

In his professional life, Bing controlled this side of himself. He came across as a charming, affable man, yet at home, he subjected his four sons to thrice-weekly brutal beatings. His alcoholic wife was kept behind closed doors, a dark secret never to be let out lest it spoil his carefully calculated image.

The four Crosby boys continued to suffer long after they stopped living under their father's roof. Their lives were marred by alcoholism, drug addiction, manic depression and—for two of them—suicide. Ultimately, where did all the pain come from?

Many years after Bing had built another family with his second wife, Kathryn, he told an interviewer that he left the role of disciplinarian to her because he thought he might have been too strict with the first four. That was as close to an apology as Gary ever got . . . and even then, it was delivered to an interviewer, not to him.

Today, at fifty-nine, Gary continues to pursue his greatest loves: singing and acting. He jokes that he is on his fourteenth comeback, "and that's not easy for a guy who's never been there!"

GARY CROSBY

I was the most violent son-of-a-bitch on the face of the earth. It started when I was a kid waiting for the beating; the fear I felt sitting there waiting for the roof to come down on me was enough to drive anyone to violence. And when I exploded, I erupted like a volcano.

Our home was like something out of *Oliver*. In the morning we were supposed to get up at seven o'clock. We slept two in a room. Our housekeeper was allowed to whip us. She would stand between our rooms at 6:55 and if she heard us whispering, she came in and whipped us with a wire hanger. If we left anything in our rooms before or after school, the next day we had to wear that item to school on a piece of string around our neck, even if it was a pair of underwear or a sock. Humiliation. My dad used to take us to school and say to the teachers, "If they do anything wrong, you give it to them, phone me, and when they get home, I'll give it to them." That's how it went.

My mother was an alcoholic, but we were never allowed to say she had been drinking. Our mother was "asleep." Our mother had a "headache." Our mother was "just resting." Sometimes she was "just resting" in the middle of the hallway. My mother was a sweet, gentle soul. But when she was drinking she was a monster; one of those old-time girls who believed the husband was always right. It tore her ass up to see us being beaten. Sometimes she would whip us to keep him from whipping us so brutally. She would say, "Do you want to wait until your father gets back or do you want it from me?" We'd say, "We want it from you, Mom." She'd say, "Get me a peach tree switch," and we'd pick a limb off a tree that was limber. She'd have us roll up our pants and she'd whip us on our legs. She went crazy if we moved or cried, so we'd have to stand real still. But I know Mom loved us.

When my mother was drinking, Dad would have a doctor come to the house every day to talk to her for one hour. She would sit there white-knuckling it, trying to stay sober until the doctor came. The minute Dad went on the road, the doctor stopped coming and Mom got drunk. Dad was friggin' mystified. He'd say, "Man, this is the best guy around. I pay him all this money and we can't figure out what's wrong?" Dad just didn't get it.

My brothers got a beating once a week. I got two a week, sometimes three. Dad used to give it to us with a Western leather belt that had little silver points sticking out. He'd take our pants down and then methodically, and very calmly, he would whip us till we bled. After he stopped, we'd go into the bathroom and look at our asses in the mirror. When we got older he used a chain or a cane with a big knob at the end. He'd hold it with two hands like a baseball bat, bend us over and then step into us fourteen or fifteen times.

I couldn't yell back, so I made it a game. From the time I was little I'd say, "I'm going to try to look back at him while he's doing it." Finally I got to where I could stand there bent over, look back over my shoulder, and stare at him while he was whipping me. Afterwards I'd go to my room and jump up and down grabbing my ass. But while he was doing it, I would just stare him in the fucking eyes. When I'd look into his eyes, I'd see nothing—just boredom and dissatisfaction.

I got an extra beating every week because the old man didn't like the size of my ass. He used to say, "You're going to be a fat kid and I'm not going to let you." He would arbitrarily pick a weight which I would have to match every Tuesday night at six o'clock. If I missed it by a quarter of a pound, I'd get a whipping. If I made it, I'd set up a binge-purge thing. The other kids got whatever they wanted to eat, but I only got grapefruit and red meat. So, I ran around the house stealing everything I could eat for the next few days. By the weekend, I'd be up five pounds. Then I would steal all the laxatives in the medicine chest so that by Tuesday night I'd be the correct weight.

I was a speed freak before I was an alcoholic. Amphetamines were just getting popular. I'd come home with a box full of pills and suddenly I was smiling and laughing all the time. My teeth were clenched together, my eyes were bugging out of my head, and I was talking at 78 rpms; but the old man thought I was happy because I was losing weight.

When I was small, Dad used to take me to the studios and the racetrack, places where he was a big shot. I don't know why he took me. Maybe he was trying to do the family man image thing. I'd have to sit around with people like Bob Hope, Dean Martin, Jerry Lewis, big shots from Paramount. I wasn't allowed to talk; I'd just sit quietly in the corner and he would say to me, "Hey, satchel-ass! Bucket-butt! Go to my dressing room and get me my pipe." All his pals would laugh and I'd just grin and go and get the pipe. He made me smile so I wouldn't look like a bad sport. When I'd get back, he'd hold me in front of them, turn me around and say, "Look at the ass on that kid. Got an ass like a pastry cook." They all thought it was the funniest thing in the world. That's the stuff that still hurts.

Those were the times I really thought about murdering him. While he was talking and those people were laughing at me I had fantasies of taking a knife and ripping him from his balls clean up to his throat. I'd just sit there and dream stuff like that—cutting his throat, shootin' him, throwin' him off a cliff . . . whatever the fuck I could possibly do to him. I'd plan how I could do it and get away with it. That's how bad it got. Meanwhile, the public was reading that he took his son fishing and hunting and on all these wonderful, American-dream activities.

I can look in the mirror now and still see that fat kid sitting there. When I quit playing sports and went into business, I went from a solid 215 pounds to 163. I dropped three sizes, but all that negative stuff had been pounded into my brain and I couldn't see any difference. So I continued to try to lose weight.

When I got beaten as a child, I thought it was because I was fat and ugly and didn't have talent. I felt I couldn't do anything. I thought I deserved the abuse because I couldn't keep all the rules. On top of that, when I was little, people would cross the street and run up to the car to tell me how much they loved him, how much he'd done for them, and how his singing had helped their lives, how hearing him on the radio was wonderful, that he was the most loved man in the world. They loved him and he loved them. I couldn't love him and he couldn't love me, so I thought I was the bad guy. I had to be the bad guy, I thought it had to be me. Who else was it?

All I did from morning to night was try to plug the holes in the dam by keeping all the rules; because if one got broke, I was going to get hurt. So I tried, but I could never keep them all.

I remember one particular day when I was sitting home waiting to get whipped for the thousandth time. I remember the fear, the anxiety, the turning stomach, and getting so fucking angry at being scared that the emotions fused. I was more angry at being scared than I was about the whipping. From that time forward, every time I got scared I got violently angry.

That's what colored my life. As far back as I can remember, I've lived with homicidal anger which scared everyone away from me. It probably scared me out of the business because I got really bad with a lot of people. I went to every kind of psychiatrist I could, and we could never get to the bottom of it.

When I finally went to AA, all I had to do was get to a place where I could say, "Folks, all my life I've been scared to fuckin' death." Every time I'd say how scared I was, another layer of anger went away. It was all fear-based.

My brothers were in bad shape as well. All the years of abuse took their toll. We were all screaming for help and understanding in our own way. One time I talked to Dad about Lindsay's depression. He said, "What the hell is a manic-depressive?" I tried to explain it to him and he looked me in the eye, and not a beat went by, and he said, "Tell me something," and honest to God he meant this, "How does anybody have a mental problem?" I looked at him and suddenly it became very clear to me that everything had always gone exactly how he wanted it his whole life. He never had to overcome tragedy or difficulty. His talent was God-given and it was perfect and it was true. He had a great personality that he put on for people and he won their hearts over immediately. He was genuinely baffled about Lindsay. About Mom, about all of it.

I drank alcoholically for nearly fifteen years. I quit for the wrong reasons, and when I did, I thought I didn't need a program. I was a tough guy, I could do it on my own. So for the next nineteen years I was what they call a white-knuckle, dry drunk. I didn't drink booze. I didn't take speed. But I was still raging all the time. I tried what I thought might be solutions: religion, psychiatry, psychology, just about every self-help kind of thing. Nothing worked. I just kept getting madder. Then I started to isolate myself.

Finally, in 1981, I wound up on the operating table. I had a triple bypass at forty-eight. Before the operation the doctor told me, "You're here for two reasons: smoking and anger. How many times a day do you get angry?" I was bein' real cute and I said, "Well, Doc, I'll tell ya. When I wake up in the morning, I know I'm gonna have to fight somebody. I just wait to see who it is." He explained that I was killing myself and that if I didn't change, even with the operation . . . I'd be dead in three years.

Lying on the operating table, like a baked chicken, my body shaved and with that iodine stuff all over me, I made a deal with God. "Get me through this operation and I'll find out what this guy means about altering the attitude." I must have made about 150 promises to God in my life and never kept any of them. For some reason I kept this one. After this operation, I came back to Los Angeles to get help. A doctor referred me to a woman. She said, "You know something, Gary? You're too angry. You're going to have to go to AA." Well, as soon as I walked into my first meeting, feelings came over me; I knew I was home. I hadn't had a drink for a long time before I walked through those doors. I thought AA was just about quitting drinking. I discovered it's about finding a way to live.

I had three brothers. All four of us became alcoholics. We all drank to escape reality because our childhood was a living hell. Of my brothers, Phil and I are the only ones alive today. Lindsay died December 11, 1989; he swallowed his rifle. Dennis died May 4, 1991; he swallowed his shotgun. Phil is doing it the long, slow, painful way. He's taking a lot of Seconal and drinking a lot of beer. He doesn't get up until about six-thirty every night. He watches television all night or goes out to some bar. He goes to bed about six-thirty in the morning. He's been divorced five times. He was abusive to his children but he won't admit it. The beat goes on.

Today I judge myself by different standards than I ever have before. By the world's standards, I'm a failure. By my new standards, I'm doing okay. I don't drink today, one day at a time. What's even more remarkable is that I don't get angry. Oh, I still get pissed off sometimes, but I'm not the perpetual hot-head I used to be. Far from it. And when I look in the mirror, I don't see old "bucket butt" anymore.

People ask, "Are you angry with your father?" I say, "No." The man's dead. I stopped being angry at him the minute I could get out from under him and he couldn't hurt me anymore.

An interesting thing happened the other day. A guy called me to do an interview for a documentary on the old man. Usually, I don't do those things, but I'm changing. I decided to work on the program and I found I could talk about an area of life with him that was actually very good. My father was a pleasure to work with. He was the best. Best tone. Everybody said he was the best singer. He would make you feel like there was no problem. If you goofed, he'd make a goof right behind you so they had to start to tape again. He'd clown around and put you at ease, not just with us, but I'm talking about with everybody. I was able to at least say this.

I feel like a survivor, but I don't take any joy in being the only one. I'm happy I made it through, that I am who I am today. I'm sorry it took what it took to get here. I accept responsibility for that. If I had my life to do over again, I'd do it a whole different way. But I know I'm a better man. I stopped the legacy of abuse in my family, a fact of which I'm proud.

If anybody identifies with my story, if anybody out there thinks he's worthless or feels she's no good, I'd say, "Take it from me: You're not as bad as you think you are, not nearly. You're probably not bad at all—no matter how often your parents might have told you or shown you that you were. You do make a difference in this world. Have faith and trust—close your eyes and walk on through. There is a way out of an abusive childhood—and I'm not talking about the route my brothers took. Look for the good in yourself. It's there. I guarantee it. Just don't give up."

*It's what you learn
after you know it all
that counts.*

TRUMAN CAPOTE

Sally Marr

LENNY BRUCE'S MOTHER. *The title sounds like an oxymoron. Could Lenny Bruce, the iconoclastic and notorious stand-up comedian, really have had a mother? Of course he did, and once you've met the woman herself—Sally Marr—you can begin to get an idea of the kind of home life that spawned a sense of humor like Lenny Bruce's.*

Sally Marr, the first female stand-up comic in America, was eighty-five years old when I met her. She behaves like a much younger woman. She has tremendous energy and a sharp memory, though many of her memories are not pleasant.

As a child, Sally was by turns neglected and abused, both verbally and physically. Her mother was mentally unstable. Today she would probably be diagnosed as a paranoid schizophrenic. Sally's early years were completely colored by her mother's mood swings and fears. The instability and abuse took its toll: two of Sally's brothers suffered nervous breakdowns, and a third committed suicide.

Sally escaped her erratic home through a hasty teenage marriage. She married a man who wound up neglecting her the few times he was home between long periods of abandonment.

Besides her own indominable spirit, her son, Lenny, was her only source of happiness. When she lost him to a drug overdose in 1966, it was the toughest moment she had faced in a very tough life.

A beloved member of the comedy community to this day, Sally has sought and found solace in the laughter she creates through comedy.

119

SALLY MARR

*L*OOKING back I realize I grew up in a pretty crazy household; but when you're a kid, whatever way you're living is all you know. So how was I to tell that my home life wasn't quite like everyone else's?

My parents were Russian immigrants. They came to this country by boat with four children. I was the only one born here, in Jamaica, Long Island, on December 30, 1906.

Ever since I can remember, my mother suffered from fits of anger. You didn't need to provoke her; she could fly off at any moment. No one ever knew what set her off. I might be sound asleep. Next thing I knew there she was pulling my hair, screaming that I loved my Aunt Mema, her sister-in-law, better than her. She'd rip the furniture with knives. She threw things at me—whatever was handy—boiling coffee, knives, dishes. I hid under the bed because she was always yelling and hitting me. She was such an angry person. I tried so hard to win her favor, but it never worked. I'd say, "Hey, look, Ma. I ironed all these shirts." Then, WHACK. She'd slap me a good one. I would wonder what I had done.

No one ever visited. Our house was always a mess. By the time I was nine years old, I was doing almost all of the cooking and laundering. Sometimes I'd find a chicken in the bureau drawer and I'd wonder what could have possessed my mother to put it there. Of course, I would never ask. Nobody talked to me, anyway.

That was the thing about life at our house. Even the few times something did strike you as crazy or at least a little odd, you never talked about it. You never said a word for fear it would only stir up my mother.

Neighbors called the police at least three times a week. My parents were always fighting. From outside it always sounded as if someone were about to be killed. I slept in my clothes in case I had to run to my Aunt Mema's in the middle of the night to get help. The only quiet nights we knew were when they held my mother for observation. But they always let her go because she wasn't "crazy enough," meaning she could carry on a conversation.

No one took care of my basic needs. When I was a kid, I loved to roller-skate. I roller-skated everywhere I had to go, so the soles of my shoes never got worn. Because they weren't worn out, my father never bought me new shoes. My feet began to grow all twisted and bent until I figured out what the problem was.

It was the same way with my teeth. My Aunt Mema owned a candy store, so I was always eating candy. I got hyperactive from all the sugar and my teeth were rotting in my head. But no adult ever warned me about the connection. By the time I figured it out for myself, it was too late for my teeth.

I didn't have any friends. I changed schools constantly because my mother was always showing up to start a ruckus. She'd barge into my classroom shouting, "You whore! You son-of-a-bitch! You like your father more than you like me!" All the kids would stare at me; I'd be too embarrassed ever to go back. It's why I never went past the third grade; my mother always found me.

I always tried to hide how much my mother's behavior hurt me. My Aunt Mema used to say, "You should never tell your troubles to anybody." I took that to mean she didn't want to hear either; so I didn't tell anyone. I just kept my mouth shut. I just wanted people to like me. I think that's how I first developed my sense of humor. I literally learned how to dance just so I could please people. I thrived on the applause.

My brother, Irving, encouraged me. He took me into New York City a few times to go to clubs and dance contests. He was the first person to tell me I was funny. It was on one of those trips to New York that I met Mickey Schneider. Mickey was my brother's girlfriend's brother. Four weeks after we met, Mickey—then on the rebound from another girlfriend—proposed to me. Four weeks after that, we got married. I was thrilled; I couldn't believe I would be getting out of my crazy house.

Mickey left me on our wedding night. He kept coming and going for the next seven years.

When he was around, he was miserable. Sometimes he wouldn't speak to me for months. When he did talk, it was usually to complain about what an embarrassment my mother was. And this whole time, I believed I didn't deserve any better. I felt guilty about my mother. I figured Mickey was right. It was years before I had enough self-esteem to realize how badly he treated me.

Mickey never wanted to have children. When I got pregnant, he forced me to have an abortion. I was seventeen. It was the most horrible thing I'd ever been through. When I got pregnant a second time, I almost killed myself. Instead, Mickey made me get another abortion. He was away for most of my third pregnancy. When he finally showed up, I told him I was going to have the baby. Leonard Alfred Schneider was born October 13, 1925. Mickey told me he would never like children; he never did like Lenny.

Needless to say, Lenny didn't exactly know a stable family life. I'd like to think he didn't have it as bad as I'd had it as a kid. But for all intents and purposes, he never really had a father. And I wasn't exactly your basic apple-pie mom. But we were pals, best friends. We talked about everything and he developed a great sense of observation during these years.

I never realized what a romantic Lenny was and how much a part of him must have missed having a more traditional home growing up until one time when he was on leave from the Navy. We were out together at a big party and he asked me to dance with a friend of his. I said okay and a man in uniform stepped up. We started dancing. After a moment I realized the guy was Mickey, Lenny's dad. I was furious with Lenny for pulling such a stunt and I looked over at him. He was crying. I'd never realized that he'd had old-fashioned fantasies about having a real family until then. It was the saddest moment of my life.

Lenny died when he was thirty-nine years old. I never turned to drugs the way Lenny did. I also never felt I had to forgive him. He never did anything that was offensive to me. If he wanted to destroy his life, it was his life. I never felt responsible for his life. And afterward, I couldn't sit and dream about what Lenny could've done. I didn't think, "Oh, Lenny, if only . . . you could have been so big . . . now I'm broke and raising your nine-year-old child." That's not who I am. What am I gonna get if I grieve? What am I gonna get if I'm angry, if I'm depressed? People don't give a shit about your depression. They have their own crap going. That's how I dealt with everything.

Years ago a Broadway play triggered interest in Lenny's life. Bob Fosse called me to arrange a meeting with him and Dustin Hoffman. The morning of the meeting I was raped. A guy broke into my apartment, put a gun to my head, his dick where he wanted it, and said, "If you scream, I'll kill you." I said, "Scream? I'm having the best time I ever had in my life." Then I did the same thing I used to do when my mother was at her craziest: I just went someplace else. That guy may have had my body, but my mind was far, far away.

I decided not to call the police because I thought it would look like a publicity stunt. I could see the headlines: "Lenny Bruce's Mother Raped."

Four hours later I was with Dustin Hoffman. "You'll never believe what happened to me today." I told him about the rape. I made it sound like a joke. He couldn't believe I hadn't canceled the meeting with him. I said, "I had an appointment, didn't I?" Then I added, "I really don't give a crap about the rape, but afterwards he went into the kitchen and stole my lamb chops, which made me mad because I hate to grocery shop."

Dustin said, "If this had happened to my mother, she would not be telling jokes; she'd be in the insane asylum." I said, "Let me tell you something. All my life there was nobody to go to, nobody to talk to. If I had had somebody to talk to, I'd probably be in the nuthouse too."

I've led such an exciting life by just getting up in the morning and thinking, "What am I gonna do today?" I adopted that philosophy because I never knew what tomorrow would bring. I don't have any regrets. I'm the luckiest woman in the world.

So maybe my way of coping isn't the healthiest, but it works for me. It's kind of like that old W. C. Fields joke. When asked whether he'd rather be dead or in Philadelphia, he replied, "On the whole, I'd rather be in Philadelphia." Well, the same goes for me. Given the choice between going nuts or telling jokes, on the whole I'd rather have a good laugh.

A CHILD

It's okay to be a child tonight, my love
  Weak and tired in my arms
  Too weary to hold up your head.
  Be the way you feel, my love
  Give in to your tears!
  Let go! The enemy's gone
  And I am here
      To muss your hair
      And stroke your skin
      And hold you close against my breasts.

It's okay to be a child tonight, my love
  No battles to win or worlds to conquer
  Not strong and powerful.
  Let me be whatever you need, my love
  Give in to your pain
  Let go! The enemy's gone.
  And only I am here
      To hold you
      And fondle you
      And love you like a child.

It's okay to be a child tonight, my love
  I already know the man
      You scream him so
      And drive him so
  But don't hide the child from me
  Let him appear—in my arms—without fear
  Because I already know
      And love you.

SUZANNE SOMERS
from *Touch Me*, © 1973

Thomas "Hollywood" Henderson

FANS OF THOMAS HENDERSON *remember him as "Hollywood" Hender-son, renegade defensive star of the Dallas Cowboys. His sensational talents on the athletic field carried him to three Super Bowls. His flamboyant style off the field set new records in the fast lane of glitzy nightclubs and beautiful women. He played in Super Bowl X at twenty-two, his first season in the NFL.*

But Thomas had no preparation for the fame and fortune he so suddenly achieved. Underneath the full-length fur coats and flashy cars lurked anger and confusion left from the brutal beatings and the violence he lived with as a child. Some of his anger he channeled into his bone-crushing tackles. The rest he tried to erase with sex, drugs, and alcohol. Eventually, they destroyed his professional career—but they also became his opportunity.

I was impressed by Thomas Henderson when I heard him speak at a Children of Alcoholics convention. When I learned about his past, I was overcome with sadness. Thomas was a violent man who has learned to be loving, trusting, and compassionate. Today, he is a sought-after lecturer, an author, and a drug and alcohol counselor who speaks to teens and school groups across the nation.

THOMAS "HOLLYWOOD" HENDERSON

ONE of the most shocking moments of my childhood was the night I watched my mother shoot my stepfather. I woke up when I heard the two of them fighting. They fought all the time, but this fight sounded different. Mamma was crying and screaming with a strength I'd never heard before. I heard her say, "I'm gonna kill you, motherfucker!" She sounded like she meant it.

As kids, my five brothers and sisters and I all slept in the same room. That night we were all wide awake. As the oldest—I was twelve—I felt it was my duty to see what was going on. I told my brothers and sisters to stay in the room until I got back.

My stepfather must have been beating the shit out of my mother. I'd seen her with a busted lip. I'd even seen her with a black eye. But I'd never seen her with both eyes closed and her mouth bleeding—until that night. I felt sorry for her and I was mad at my stepdad. He was drunk. But the strongest emotion I felt in seeing the two of them that way was fear.

Mamma was standing on the porch bleeding when I came out of our room. She had a .22 caliber rifle in her hands, and she had just shot my stepfather. I wanted to be part of the paint on the house. I could not believe this was happening. If it had to happen, it wasn't anything I wanted to see.

It may sound strange, but I liked my stepdad. He was a nice man. At least he was nice to me, but he was always beating up my mother. And now my mother had shot him for what he'd done.

Luckily for all of us, my stepdad didn't die. But for me, things were never the same.

It hadn't exactly been rosy before that night. My stepfather had been beating my mother on a regular basis, about two or three times a month. Usually, when she got beaten by him, she ended up beating my ass before the week was out. I guess she had to whip somebody just to get out her own frustrations. As the eldest, I was chosen.

My mamma never needed much of a reason to give it to me. She'd say, "What did I tell you to do? Didn't I tell you to clean that living room?" Even if I'd tried to clean up, it was never to her satisfaction. She beat me until there were welts on my arms and back. As a little boy, seven, eight, nine, I used to go for walks after her beatings. I'd be crying these little hiccup cries and I'd talk to God. I'd ask, "God, why does she do this to me?" I thought it was my fault. I'd go home and clean up the whole kitchen. I'd get the dirty diapers and wash them by hand. I'd sweep the yard. I only wanted to do good. I just wanted to please my mother, but I never could.

I now know that a lot of our problems then were beyond my control. My mother had me when she was fifteen years old. My natural father was long gone by the time I was born. My mother had had a rough childhood. She wasn't brought up by her parents. My mamma and her sister were raised by a very distant cousin named Nettie Mae. When I was old enough to wonder about my real father, I asked my mother about him. "Mamma, where is he?"

She wouldn't answer.

"What does he look like?"

She'd say, "Go look in a mirror."

So from an early age, I reminded her of my father, who wasn't exactly a guy she'd be happy to see.

When I was getting whipped, that's about the most attention I ever received. I wanted to play sports—basketball or baseball. I wanted to run track. But I had no one to encourage me. I was the oldest, so it was just assumed that I would help raise the other kids. Mamma was always telling me I was never going to amount to anything. "That boy ain't going to be shit," was her refrain. I got the message fast: I was worthless, useless; I couldn't do anything right.

As if that weren't enough, I had an uncle who said I'd be gay. Being gay is not a bad thing, but when my uncle used to tell me this back in 1964 when I was ten years old, he didn't mean it kindly.

There was never anyone for me to talk to. I never got anything close to nurturing, and ever since the night my mother shot my stepfather, I lived in absolute fear of her. I was afraid that she would kill me and it was a legitimate fear. My mother shot my grandfather five times after he pistol-whipped her. She shot a couple of other people. I don't think she was crazy. I think alcohol made her violent.

My mother and my stepfather went to work Monday through Friday at their meager-paying jobs. On the weekends, they came home with two brown sacks: one long, one short. The long one had a fifth of vodka or gin. The short one had a pint of whiskey or bourbon. This was what they looked forward to each week. It's what they lived for.

I don't remember exactly when I started drinking. When you grow up in an alcoholic home, you don't think too hard about drinking. It's so all-pervasive, you just accept it like the living-room couch. With so much liquor around all the time, it's never long before some adult invites you to have a sip or offers you a whole beer.

I think I first got really drunk when I was around ten or eleven. A friend and I chugged a pint of whiskey. I didn't like the feeling; in fact, I hated it. For many years after, I didn't drink because I knew what alcohol had done to my mother and stepfather. Instead, I smoked marijuana and took hallucinogens and speed. When I finally got around to drinking again, I'd go to a club and drink Tom Collinses. I was more interested in how many cherries I got and the orange slice than I was in the actual alcohol. But in the end, I would up being a full-blown, quart-of-gin-a-day alcoholic—just like my mom and stepdad.

At the age of eleven, I was sexually abused by a woman neighbor of ours. She started screwing me and we continued that way for about two years. At the time, I thought it was a great deal. I didn't think it had a negative effect on me until much later on when I was in treatment; only then did I realize I'd been abused. People tend not to call it abuse when little boys are introduced to sex this way at such an early age, but that's what it is. By the time I knew what sex was, I was already screwing. My whole approach to sex started with that very distorted beginning. It was many years before I came to understood how sex could truly be a way of making love.

When I was sixteen, I left my mother to go live with Nettie Mae, the distant cousin who had raised her. I still loved my mother, but I was just too afraid of her to stick around. So I moved from Austin, Texas to Oklahoma. I became "Mr. Perfect." I worked six hours a day, went to night school, and started wearing wing-tipped shoes. I drove trucks for a mail contractor on the post office docks. I'd gotten out of Austin just in time. Right before I left, one of my best friends had been killed in an accident with a gun we had stolen, and I knew it was time to get out of town. I moved away and because of this move, I went from being a little street felon to driving a 1966 Ford Galaxy 500 in 1970. I had a better car than my mom and stepdad.

I'd always played football, but I couldn't play my junior year because of a rule: if you moved from Texas to Oklahoma or vice versa without your parents, you had to sit out a year. So the only choice I had was to work. But as soon as I could play, I was back on the field again.

Once I got on that football field, I took on all the characteristics of my mother when she was drunk. I was violent. I just wanted to go out there and beat the shit out of everybody, and I did. People started calling me "The Wild Man." I had a lot of anger and playing football hard was how I got rid of it.

I've heard it said, be careful what you wish for: it may come true. I played football my senior year of high school and five years later I was in the National Football League. My first year in the NFL, I played in the Super Bowl. I was twenty-two years old: ten years removed from watching my mother shoot my stepfather, five years from leaving home. My teammates started calling me "Hollywood" because I wore full-length fur coats in the summertime. I was right where I dreamed I'd be.

But my success had no guts. I didn't feel I deserved it. It was hollow, because in my mind I was still a worthless bastard whose father had abandoned him and whose mother had beaten him every chance she had. The only difference between me and a stray dog was that I didn't have a tail to tuck between my legs.

During this time, my first brush with success, my real father looked me up. His arrival triggered a lot of very painful memories. I was happy to finally meet this man, but I also felt ashamed. I remember thinking, "Where the fuck have you been for twenty-two years?" But I didn't know how to share that. I never said anything like that to him. I just acted like it was great to know him, but deep in my heart where I lived, I hurt.

If I partied enough, I could forget all that. I could forget that I was worthless. I could forget I was a bastard. I could forget I lived in fear that my mother might one day come after me with a gun, and this is after having the success with the Cowboys and having women all over me—thousands of them. When I hear people like Wilt Chamberlain or Magic Johnson talking about their exploits, I understand. When you're a top athlete, you can have anybody you want. Screwing became a sport. So between cocaine, alcohol, and all the sex, I was able to numb that sense of worthlessness I felt to my core. It worked for a while. Then I needed more cocaine, more booze, and more sex for it to keep doing the same trick. And then I needed still more after that.

My progression was spiraling. Cocaine first took me to fancy, flashy places: clubs packed out with lots of glamorous Hollywood stars. In the end, it took me to closets. I became so paranoid through use of the drug, I hid in closets wondering who it was who was coming after me. I didn't know who it was, but I knew someone was there. Freebasing turned my lungs black. I spit up phlegm.

By the time Super Bowl XIII rolled around—Cowboys versus the Steelers—I was deeply addicted to cocaine. I got high before the game; that was my ritual. But by the third quarter, I knew I needed more. Everybody knew I had terrible sinus problems, so I knew it wouldn't cause any talk when I pulled out my nasal inhaler and took several big snorts. There on the field, in front of eighty million TV viewers, I snorted liquid cocaine.

I wanted to die, yet who could imagine it? There I was. I seemed to have it all. I understand guys like Freddie Prinze, John Belushi, and Marvin Gaye. A drug like cocaine gives you some great moments. Then all you want are a few more great moments. Then it gets so you want your whole life to be nothing but a string of those great moments. It's in that quest that you lose yourself and your soul.

My addictions took me to a point where I ended up freebasing cocaine with a teenage girl in an apartment in Long Beach, California. I was charged with sexual misconduct. At that point, I knew it was over. I knew that I was done. I knew it was time for me to stick the gun in my mouth and blow the top of my head off. There was no other choice. At least I didn't feel like there was at the time.

An attorney took me to a treatment center in Orange County, California, where I met Dr. Joseph Pursch. He treated me free of charge and sent me on a journey of healing I'm still on today. He was one of the first doctors to institute something called family week. My family couldn't come to meetings, but I had wonderful people to play their parts. I would do "empty chair" work, getting my feelings off my chest even if I was only talking to an empty chair, just pretending it was my mother or another relative in it. That was the beginning of my understanding who I was, what I was, and what had caused me to act the way I acted. It started my healing. I realized then what I had to do. Above all else I had to stay sober. If I didn't stay sober, I couldn't feel the pain. If I couldn't feel that pain, shame, and sense of worthlessness that had driven me to drink and do drugs in the first place, I wouldn't ever get past it. And I'd probably drink and do drugs again. It was that simple. This was 1983. I haven't had a drink or taken a drug since then.

I've done extensive work in therapy, psychotherapy, and group work since I got sober. I'm in the men's movement. I work in the addiction recovery field. I'm still in therapy today because I'd rather be green and growing than ripe and rotten. Today I look at myself in the mirror and I'm proud of who I see.

I've never been bad, I know I've done some bad things when I was using. Today when I meet a woman, one of the first things I say is, "I'm a nice man." She may look at me like I'm crazy, but I've had to work at being a nice man. And it's one of the best things I can say about myself today.

One of the greatest joys of my new life is raising my daughter. Thomesa lives with her mother for most of the year, much to my regret. But she lives with me for three months every summer. She's twelve years old today, the same age I was when my mother shot my stepfather. I love her with all my heart. I have put everyone on notice: no one touches my daughter. She goes to a private school, and recently they sent out a form asking for permission to physically spank students as a form of punishment. My reaction was, "Of course not." I called them and put them on notice about that right away.

Four years ago, my daughter came to spend the summer with me. She made me angry about something. I started to chase her and she ran. She hovered in the corner and put up her hands like I was going to kill her. I sat on the floor and started to cry. She asked me what was wrong and I told her she reminded me of me when I was a little boy. We went back downstairs and lay in the middle of the floor. I said, "I need to say something to you. I'm your father and I love you with all my heart. Today, I want to make a pledge to you: I have never hit you or spanked you and I want you to know I never will. I want you always to have the freedom to talk to me, to challenge me, to share your feelings with me. You can tell me when you're hurting; I'll never make fun of you." I freed her. She's really tested me a few times since then, but I've never broken my promise. And she knows she can always talk to me.

When I look back, I wonder, would I do it all the same way because of what I learned? Is this what I had to go through to understand? Initially, I'd say no way, I'd change it. Then I think, does the pain make the pleasure worth it? And I think, yeah. Today I have gotten in touch with the little Thomas and he's okay because now the adult Thomas is okay. I've accepted all that has happened. I've accepted all that I've done and I like the man that I've become. *I am not my disease.* I am not my abuse. I am not my mistakes. I am who I've become. That's the thing I'd like to end with—I'm a nice man and a nice father. Forget the whales; save the males.

Recently I received a letter from a friend who is also in recovery.

It said, "I asked for a power that I may have praise of men. I was given weakness that I may feel the need of God. I asked for all things that I may enjoy life." Today I realize that I was given life that I might enjoy all things. I have nothing I asked for but everything I hoped for, almost despite myself. My unspoken prayers were answered. I am, among all, most richly blessed.

BROKEN TOYS

Such a pretty little face
With a heart that's been torn
Living in a borrowed space
From the moment she was born
How many times she's cried
But never tears of joy
Someone's taken a little girl
And made a broken toy.

Broken toys
Lord, who will mend these broken toys
For every one we break
A broken life takes its place
That one day will break toys of its own
Oh, Lord, we've got to mend these
broken toys.

Two sad little eyes
Painted heartbreak blue
The simplest of his dreams
Have never come true
Someone else's pain
Fell on this little boy
Someone's taken a soldier
And made a broken toy.

GLORIA THOMAS,
GARY HARRISON,
AND J.D. MARTIN

Judy Mitchell

JUDY MITCHELL IS A bookkeeper with her own business in Palm Springs, California. She was physically abused by her alcoholic father throughout her childhood. Today she has put the pieces of her life back together. She is happily married to her third husband and works tirelessly as a volunteer for children of alcoholics.

JUDY MITCHELL

*T*HE memories of my childhood are filled with violence and fear. My father was a binge drinker. He'd stay away drinking one or two days or a week and come home in a vile temper. My mother would yell at him, nag him, and torment him while my older sister and I hid, terrified. We begged her to leave him alone, but she wouldn't. The next thing we'd know, he'd be beating her up. We would cry and scream while he split her lip or gave her a black eye.

I was about four or five the first time my father hit me. We had just gotten wall-to-wall carpeting and I accidentally spilled nail polish on it. I made it even worse when I tried to clean it off. I managed to hide it for a few days, but when he found it, he was furious. He rolled up the newspaper and hit me over the head and on my back at least ten times. A short time later, he began to use wire hangers up and down the back of my body. I learned to hide all the welts.

His punishments were always much more than the crime deserved. He never punished my sister and me for the major mistakes, I think because he was afraid he'd kill us. We never knew what was going to set him off, when he was going to strike. So, I was nervous all the time. I couldn't write without gripping the pencil, I could never go to the bathroom and I shook all the time.

We moved constantly all through my grade school years because my parents were always separating. But my father would tell Mom that she couldn't get along without him, and eventually she'd believe him and he'd come back to live with us. When he was around, playing was not allowed in our household. We were supposed to come directly home from school and never do anything. We were never allowed to participate in any school activities. We were latchkey kids, having been left at home alone from the time we were about six and seven.

Dad picked on me more because I was the rebel. You always had to do as he wanted. If you didn't, there was a price to pay. He didn't punish my sister half as much because she was more willing to do everything he said. Once, years later, he confessed to me that he was more afraid of her—of the love that was there. I think my dad knew that I would always love him. I hated him. I loved him. I could never win his approval. I could never do enough. I could never do the things I wanted, to play, to have a good time.

When he came after me, I wouldn't attempt to hit him back. I ran and tried to get away. I would scream and cry and beg. I would jump up and down. Sometimes I would wet my pants, begging, "Daddy, Daddy, please don't hit me. Please don't!"

He always hit me on the back. When it was over, he'd send me to my room, and I'd think, "You'll be sorry when I die." Some days I wanted to kill him. I wished I could leave. Or if I had to stay, I really wanted him to go away. I liked it best when he was on his binges, even though the relief of having him gone was always accompanied by the dread of what would happen when he came back.

After the scenes and the fights, in the morning, there was always the promise of a bright future, that if everybody was good enough, we might have a wonderful family life. So the dangling carrot was always out there, that next year things would be better. It took me a long time to sort out that I was always living for a reward later in life. Of course, tomorrow never comes. I had to learn to live in the present. You can have plans for the future but you also have to have the fun, the love, the joy of today.

I found a lot of release in books. I used to read romantic novels. I still do. They were a big escape. I liked to read novels about power and people who moved away from poverty and abusive situations.

Dating was a desperate hope for love. It wasn't a whole lot of fun. On top of that, I never knew what would happen when the guy came to the front door. I didn't even know if Dad would let me go. I tried to get away before he came home, or I'd climb out my bedroom window.

Once, when I was about fifteen, I came home and found some women in the house. My father was in bed with one of them. I just looked and walked out of the room. I told Mom, hoping she would leave him for good. That was a turning point in our relationship. I guess it made me feel like I had a little power. I remember telling him, "I don't want you ever to hit me." But he did hit me one last time, when I was sixteen.

My aunt caught me in bed with my boyfriend when I was babysitting at her house. She threw us both out. When I got home my dad was waiting for me. He hit me in the face and then he left. He was gone for two months. During that time, "us girls" did all right together. When I walked in one day and found he'd come back, I yelled, "I am not living under the same roof with him!" I'd taken a stand and he never hit me again. From that point on we started to make amends in our relationship.

Because I'd always been denied any intimacy with my father, I tried to re-create it with other men. Men became my fix, an addiction for me. But, because I didn't have the faintest idea of what intimacy was, I misused my sexuality. I could have been one of those wanton women I'd been reading about all my life; I also knew that I could use sex as a way of keeping an emotional distance. Intimacy, to my mind, was always disappointing. When I was young, my relationships were never fulfilling, but I don't think I had any idea what I wanted or what I could have.

I ended up marrying a very selfish man when I was seventeen. He was controlling like my dad, but he didn't drink or physically abuse me.

I tried to be perfect. I went to church. I taught Sunday school. The house was perfect. I cooked three meals a day, worked full time, and ironed his underwear. He didn't even know where we kept the milk. While he did nothing, I kept trying to do more because I thought that was my job in life. It was very boring. He

145

didn't want me to have a life of my own, he didn't want me to have friends, and I didn't. If he came upstairs and I was reading, he would say, "All you ever do is bury your nose in books." He didn't want me to have anything. So when he came to me after seven years and told me I was boring, that he had met a girl he wanted to date and he was leaving, there was a part of me that was relieved.

I was almost twenty-five and, for the first time, I felt free. I was terrified. Then my dad died. I rarely drank when my father was alive, but right after he died I started. I guess it was inevitable. Then, just before my twenty-sixth birthday, I fell in love. He was everything I thought I needed. He was married, but separated at the time. I fell passionately in love with this man. He taught me a lot. But we had a stormy relationship. The anger was never violent, but he would leave me . . . just like Dad. I drank because I didn't know what to do about the hurt and the pain and the anger. I was probably an alcoholic within a year, if that long.

I started drinking heavily and I wanted to die of depression. I was thirty by that time. That stormy relationship ended. He married another girl six weeks after we broke up. A couple of years later I married a man who was really nice and who took care of me. But I never really got over that other guy.

During the first few months of my second marriage, we lived in Newport on the beach. My husband would come home with two six-packs of beer and I would drink every day. I got so I couldn't leave the house. I couldn't even go out on the beach.

When I was drinking, I was terribly hostile. It was the only time I ever allowed myself to be angry; I would get drunk and be angry. I was very verbally abusive, vicious. I attacked. It didn't matter who you were or where you were. I would rake you over the coals. I think my childhood was so out of control that as an adult, I wanted to control everyone. That's a part of me that was probably a whole lot like my father.

The last night of my drinking, I called my "true love" while I was in a blackout. I woke up with the phone in my hand and no memory of what I'd done. That was so totally demoralizing to me that I went to AA meetings.

Over the years, I've learned that I'm okay, I'm a good person, that I'm not stupid. That was a big one. My dad had often told me I was stupid. When *he* quit telling me, *I* told me I was stupid. I needed that negative reinforcement because I would not allow myself anything good.

I didn't have a normal childhood. I don't know if there is a normal childhood, compared to the storybooks. I had to learn how to reach out, how to listen, how to discover what else is available. I'm not ashamed of what I've done. It's taken a lot of years and I still cry for the little girl I lost. It wasn't until I was forty that I learned how to share my thoughts and dreams and desires with a man. I'm in my third marriage and I'm just learning how to do that; I still struggling with it.

I've learned that I'm worth something; that I have some value. I've learned to do the best I can and whatever happens, happens. I started my own business about ten years ago. I have a lot of courage now.

Today, I am at peace, most of the time. Life has challenges. If it was perfect and I was on that smooth thing, I would slide all over the place. It has its ups and downs. I like it this way. I like the idea of adventure.

The way is smooth,
why do you throw rocks
in front of you?

ZEN PROVERB

Vicki Hufnagel

VICKI HUFNAGEL IS THE *renowned gynecologist who pioneered laser surgery to remove fibroid tumors from the uterus. The procedure, which involves the consequent reconstruction of the uterus, represents a medical watershed for women. Prior to Hufnagel's development of this procedure, the standard treatment for fibroid tumors was a hysterectomy.*

The author of No More Hysterectomies, *Hufnagel has become an advocate for women's rights and women's health issues. She works tirelessly to effect legislation on women's behalf.*

Hufnagel rose against nearly impossible odds to become a doctor. She grew up in a very poor family, raised by physically abusive parents who were no more than children themselves. Early on she learned to rely on her "warrior within" to remove herself first from her abusive parents and then from their legacy.

VICKI HUFNAGEL

/Ⅵ\Y parents were very young when they had me: my mother was sixteen, my father was nineteen. They both abused alcohol and drugs. By the time I was six or seven years old, they were abusing me. I was violently battered by my mother on a routine basis at least twice a week.

I really believe my mother would have been unstable even without the drugs and alcohol. Her behavior was certainly extremely erratic at all times of the day.

My mother would beat me with only the slightest provocation. She'd slap me hard on the face, head, arms, and legs. She wouldn't need much of an excuse to hit me. I would be beaten if I didn't spell a word right. I was in first grade, just learning how to spell, and she would slap me any time I made a mistake. Once she fractured my skull with a broom handle.

When I got a little older, my mother got into scarring me. She had really long fingernails and she would dig them into my skin until I'd bleed. She also used belts—not the leather end, but the buckle part. That would really, really hurt. The more marks she put on me, the more she seemed to get into it.

Up until the time I was twelve or thirteen, my father was usually not home when I got hit. He would see the marks and bruises my mother put on me, but he acted as if nothing had happened. When I got older, he began to beat me also—with his fists, full force.

School became the only good thing in my life. I showed aptitude

153

at a young age. The teachers would praise me for my good work and I loved it. It was so nice to have people saying positive things about me for a change. Both my parents were also extremely abusive verbally, so I didn't get much praise at home.

My mother seemed pleased by my good grades, but once she understood how important doing well in school was to me, she used that against me. She began to devise ways of preventing me from studying. It was one of her ways of controlling me. For example, I would have a big project due in junior high or high school, a project my entire grade would depend on. I'd have a weekend to do it, but she would decide that that was the weekend I had to remove every screen in every window in the house and clean them. She was extremely exacting in terms of how I should clean those screens. She'd make it a ritual. I'd have to scrape the dirt off with a knife. Then I'd have to use a brush, then ammonia. Then I'd have to do the sliding doors and their frames and scrub them all down, too. Most times I wasn't able to finish these cleaning assignments until eight P.M. Sunday night. I'd be exhausted, but I'd have to stay up until one or two in the morning to get my schoolwork done.

If kids from school came over to play or to do homework on a class project when I was supposed to be doing housework, she'd beat me right in front of them. I wasn't allowed to stop for any reason. It made me feel ashamed, embarrassed, and angry. My parents were always embarrassing me. They were uneducated people. Neither one of them finished high school. My father met my mother when he was a jockey and she was a pretty blonde hanging around the racetrack.

The racetrack lifestyle is like a circus. You go from city to city. I must have been to fifty schools by the time I got my high-school diploma. I never had a permanent home or school until I was fifteen years old. We traveled so my father could get work, but we still never had much money. We lived on chicken pot pies or we'd go hungry. When things got really tight, my parents would send me to my grandmother's.

At this time my mother was doing Dexedrine and poppers. My father's addiction to cocaine was so bad he was almost blind. I remember getting sent to my grandmother's because he was blind for a while. They both used marijuana. All of this was accompanied by alcohol. They were always high on something.

When I was a teenager, my mother would initiate arguments with my father. She'd antagonize him until he got so angry he'd explode. He'd break things and then he'd hit her until she was bleeding or black and blue. Even though she was abusive to me, I felt a strong urge to protect my mother; but whenever I got in the middle of their fights, my father beat me also. He'd punch me in the face with his fist.

Once, when I was sixteen, I punched him back. "If you hit me one more time, I'm going to fucking kill you," I told him; then I just started punching him. He said, "Fine, but I'm going to kill you." Then he punched me again.

I left home after that, but I wound up coming back. I always came back. Somehow I always believed it would be better. I wanted so much to be a part of a family. That fantasy of a happy family life was like a drug; it pulled me back so many times.

Very early on, the warrior in me wanted to show my parents that I could make it without them. I didn't think I was better than my parents; but I never wanted to be like them, not in any way. In spite of everything, I have compassion for them, but they have never understood that about me.

I certainly didn't learn anything useful from their example. I developed a hatred for marriage. I never wanted to be a mother. I wanted to be a warrior and fight. The only aims I thought were important were to be strong, to endure, and to survive. I don't think I could have gotten through my childhood feeling any other way.

It was my idea to go to college. My parents' vision was for me to get married and live in a trailer park. Instead, I got accepted to Radcliffe on a scholarship. Even with the scholarship, I had to work three jobs to be able to pay for the dorm and other expenses. In the morning I walked horses from about four to ten. At eleven o'clock I'd go to a shopping mall to do market research. I'd do that until six, grab a quick dinner and head over to the paper factory where I'd pack plastic cups until midnight. That was the job I liked best. I could just sit there packing the cups by rote. It was like being a machine. Nobody knew anything about me. I'd sit there and think about how I was going to persevere and become a doctor.

When I got a little bit older, I wanted to fall in love; but I didn't feel I could trust anyone. I got myself into some terrible situations. I was always going out with the most dangerous men I could find—married men, men with victimizing or psychopathic behavior, men who made my father look like a wimp. Even at that time I could tell I wasn't making healthy choices. I knew I'd survived quite a lot. I'd even triumphed in certain respects. I was becoming a doctor, just as I'd always hoped I would. But even though I was a survivor, I hadn't learned the proper social dynamics. I'd never seen two people live as partners. I'd never witnessed healthy love.

In a way I had to hit bottom in the romance department before I began to get my act together. I'd fallen for a very controlling man for whom I worked. I think the thing he enjoyed most about our relationship was simply having power over me, and I participated in that for a time. After I put that relationship behind me, I made a conscious decision that nobody was going to treat me like that again.

I've been married for seven years now. My husband and I have two beautiful daughters. Within my marriage there is great respect. My husband and I value each other.

Marriage has been difficult for me because I never learned relationship skills growing up. My husband and I have had our share of problems because of it. We still have a big block at which to chip away, but we are working on our problems together. Already the block is a lot smaller than it once was, so I have a lot of reasons to hope.

Since I didn't learn good parenting from my parents, I knew I needed professional help there. I went into psychotherapy and am still in treatment. My childhood is the blueprint of my experience as a human being. There are times when my elder daughter is being difficult that I feel like hitting her or pushing her away, particularly when I'm exhausted or when my low self-esteem kicks in. My reaction is a direct result of my childhood. But I don't. I just don't do it. I would never hit her.

My father was a neglected child. My mother often raved about having been sexually abused. I was a battered child; but the cycle of abuse stops with me. I will never pass on the violence that was inflicted on me. My daughters know intimacy, warmth, and love.

My mother is no longer living. I wasn't able to reach any resolution with her before her death. I was too involved with simply trying to survive at the time. She never gave me any indication that she wanted resolution. Rather than go to the hospital where I work when she fell ill, my mother went to a hospital I wouldn't even walk into. She was misdiagnosed there three times in one week. She went home and bled to death.

I've tried to give my father every opportunity to connect, but it hasn't worked out. I feel he's made some bad choices in the last few years. He no longer sees our children. He's still not the father I would have liked him to be; but I can accept that now. I understand it and I deal with it. If I couldn't have a happy family as a child, at least I have one now as a mother.

Today I find a lot of solace in my daughters, Tara and Demitra, and in my work. There's a lot of joy in my life today; it isn't the perpetual struggle it was when I was growing up.

*Rage gives people
a way to
overcome powerlessness.*

Randy Shilts

ABUSED CHILDREN GROW UP *feeling a deep sense of shame about their abuse. That shame helps promote secrecy. The abused child is too ashamed to tell anyone what's really going on.*

Randy Shilts was burdened early on by two secrets. His first secret was about his mother. She was given to drastic mood swings and was a habitual drinker who beat Randy and his five brothers every day. Even though the beatings were often fierce, Randy was careful to hide his welts and bruises along with his feelings so that no one would ever suspect his horrible secret. Later on, Randy recognized that he was gay, which entailed keeping another secret. Given the unenlightened view of homosexuality that prevailed when he was growing up in the 1960s, Randy never disclosed his sexual preference. Through high school he got himself a girlfriend and played it straight.

Swept up by the fervor of the gay liberation movement in the early 1970s, Randy told everyone in his life—including his mother and father—that he was gay in a single day. From then on he embarked on a vocal role in the gay movement, chiefly through his work as a journalist.

In 1983 his paper, the San Francisco Chronicle, *assigned him to cover the AIDS epidemic full time. His ensuing years on the beat culminated in his 1987 best-seller,* And the Band Played On: Politics, People and the AIDS Epidemic. *Translated into six languages and released in fourteen countries, the highly acclaimed book won numerous awards. Randy was named Author of the Year by the American Society of Journalists and Authors.*

But while Randy had been able to deal openly with his sexuality, he was still silent on the subject of his abusive childhood. When he finally addressed the issue, he did so with the candor and dedication to the truth that has served him so well in his journalistic career. In so doing, he's truly been able to set himself free.

RANDY SHILTS

I'M the third of six boys with a twenty-five-year span between the oldest and the youngest.

My mother was given to horrible rages for as long as I can remember. I have clear memories of her drinking through my junior high and high school years. The alcohol really worked her up. Not only would she act crazy and get mad unpredictably, but she beat us all the time—almost every day. Not a swat on the head; she beat us with a belt. It was very ritualistic.

Other people talk about getting spanked and the embarrassment associated with it, but my mother did it to inflict pain. She made us take our pants down and stand over the toilet, so humiliation was a part of it, too; but mainly it just hurt. I can remember seeing my brother with stripes of welts all over his back from getting beaten so hard. I also remember going to school after being beaten myself on these crazy mornings and trying to act as though everything was all right. I didn't want anyone to know about my terrible secret, so I had to pretend things at home were normal.

When I was nine years old, I resolved that I wouldn't cry no matter how hard my mom beat me. To this day I can't cry. It's horrible. Crying is an expression of feelings, and I stopped feeling.

With things so tough at home, school became my escape. My teachers were substitute parents. I'd be very good in school and was always doing extra credit as a way of currying teachers' favor. In turn, I would get their approval.

When I was four or five years old, I became aware that I was different, though it took years to realize it related to my sexual identity. Nobody talked about that back then. There weren't words for it. There wasn't a sense that gay people were a minority group that deserved civil rights. So there was no one I could talk to. It was my secret alone.

By the time I was in junior high, I was keeping two horrible secrets. To my way of thinking then, both demonstrated what a bad person I was. I thought I was a bad person because I was being beaten nearly every day. Add to that this secret knowledge I had that something was unspeakably different about me, and you can begin to understand why I wanted to shut out my feelings.

My mom stopped beating me when I threatened to hit her back at age sixteen; but I felt my parents hated me. I didn't feel valued. I don't remember ever being told that I was loved through my childhood. Never once. As a child I didn't think anybody loved me.

I graduated from high school in 1969. The only time I ever heard homosexuality openly discussed was by my favorite sociology teacher. She made the statement that maybe homosexuals weren't criminals, maybe they were just sick. At the time that was a very liberal thing to say. But it still made me feel awful because by then I knew I was gay. So I hid it as best I could. I even went steady all through high school.

It wasn't until I was a sophomore in college that I began to view homosexuality in a different way. That was 1972 and the gay liberation movement was about three years old. For the first time in my life it occurred to me that I wasn't wrong; society was wrong. That was incredibly liberating. I decided I didn't want to live with this secret any more. In one day I told everybody in my life that I was gay, including my mother and my father. My father actually took it pretty well. When I told him, he said, "I always knew you were different." My mom was much more tense. Any talk of sex made her very nervous. I could tell she was uptight, but my brothers were totally supportive. Compared to living with the insanity of my mother's rages, my being gay didn't seem to be such a big deal.

I didn't drink at all until I was twenty-one. I was given to deep depressions and migraine headaches all through my early life. Marijuana was wonderful because it would pull me out. It was very much an antidepressant drug. When I turned twenty-one and came out and started going to gay bars, I became a daily marijuana smoker. The first time I ever bought my own grass, I remember thinking, "I'll never have to be depressed again." It was such a telling moment. I was looking to marijuana to solve all my problems.

Then I started drinking. I never drank to have a drink in the social sense. I drank to get drunk. I assumed everybody drank to get drunk. I mean, what else? Rapidly I became a blackout drinker. I lost my memory from the very beginning. It's amazing. I always thought alcoholics were weak people, but now I think they tend to be twice as strong. Not only do you have to maintain a normal life, but you also need more than an average supply of energy to counteract how you are depleting yourself. My last two years of college I'd be getting drunk three or four nights a week and carrying extra heavy loads of course work, on which I got almost straight A's, while also working for the campus newspaper. I was a happy drunk, charming. Toward the end I got moody, but at this point I was a happy, nice drunk.

I can look at this behavior and go back to that abused childhood, the little kid who was never going to cry again and I can see that this was the way it manifested on an unconscious level. I didn't consciously know this because I had repressed all those feelings. But I do know that when I left home, I didn't talk with my family for two or three years because there was so much anger. Later I was able to put it all out of my mind. And, once I made up with my parents, I told myself, "Well, it wasn't that bad;" and my brothers always said, "It wasn't that bad." I figured it was just me; I had dramatized it. This is typical of children of alcoholics. We minimize. Yeah, I was beaten every day, but it wasn't as bad as other people's lives. One of my brothers said, "We all survived and came out all right." Which is true. The oldest four of us are very successful professionally, but emotionally we've all had serious problems. One brother became the family juvenile delinquent and disappeared ten years ago. He must have been so pained to run like that. Maybe he was the most honest of all of us. He didn't pretend; he didn't know how to put on a happy face.

As I got older, my drinking became very pronounced. I was a

freelance writer in San Francisco through the end of the 70s for publications like the *Village Voice* and *New West Magazine.* I worked twelve to fourteen hours, six days a week; but I still found time to get drunk four or five nights a week.

In 1981 the *Chronicle* hired me, which was the job I always wanted. The *Chronicle* was wonderfully conducive for drinking. I got along well with all the other reporters. They were accepting of me and seemed to like to drink as much as I did. We'd go to reporters' bars after work and everybody would buy each other doubles. There was this warm, drunken camaraderie. So now instead of drinking at nine P.M., I was drinking at five when I got off work. After that I'd go home and drink wine with dinner. I couldn't see the danger signs. My drinking escalated like crazy.

It was around then that a number of things started happening. I began writing about AIDS. Things were getting serious. People I knew were dying, but the gay community was in denial. I started having mood changes. I was turning into a maudlin drunk or a mean drunk, because my alcoholism was progressing rapidly. In 1983 as I wrote more about AIDS, the gay community felt I was making gays look bad and that I was sensationalizing the problem to sell newspapers. I was getting criticized; and when you get criticized from your own community, it hurts a lot.

Then very suddenly my mom died of an aneurysm which I believe was alcohol-related. That triggered my last eight months of drinking. I'd get drunk every single night—real drunk. Gay community leaders had targeted me. Horrible things were being written and said about me. I couldn't go anywhere without people yelling at me, and I still had all this unprocessed grief from my mother dying. One night I went out on a dinner break and had six double Jack Daniels back-to-back. I was working the two to ten shift at the *Chronicle* and came back from a two-and-a-half-hour dinner totally drunk. That really terrified me because I'd worked so hard to overcome all this discrimination and get the job I really wanted at the *Chronicle;* and now I was going to blow it with this cheap high. That was the last time I ever had a drink. It was February 22, 1984. I still didn't understand the essence of recovery. I smoked marijuana every day and did for the next year, but in April 1985, I quit that too.

I began working on *And the Band Played On* in 1985 and couldn't sleep nights, so I started taking sleeping pills. One sleeping pill every three nights soon became one sleeping pill every night; and pretty soon it was two every night. I became addicted to sleeping pills, and I had to quit that in November of '86. Since that time I haven't used any mind-altering substances. I have become very serious about recovery. I go to support groups several times a week.

I have an addictive personality, and I think it's been about abating pain. Alcoholism runs in my family. I ascribe it to a genetic component. To me, it is very clear the reason I drank and always got drunk was to seek complete oblivion. I could pull myself away from that horrible pain that was always there in the background. I couldn't begin to live life without drugs and alcohol until I started dealing with that pain. As soon as I stopped using them, the pain started coming up—memories, horrible memories, the feeling that everybody hated me in my childhood.

Because of the fear I had of my mother's violence, I have a difficult time having any kind of personal confrontation. I cannot deal with arguments. It's been a real problem. If you can't have arguments, little things build and end up destroying relationships. But when I grew up, that was very adaptive behavior. If I talked back, I'd get hit more. It was a logical conclusion not to talk back, not to say anything, because I wouldn't get hit. Not to have a confrontation. That's how I preserved myself. Now, that's no longer adaptive.

When I got into recovery, I thought all my problems were because I was a drunk; and that's how I used to medicate the symptoms. Really, what determined me beyond anything else was growing up in this alcoholic childhood.

People don't realize what's going on in the privacy of family homes. What's never factored into juvenile delinquency are the family problems—kids growing up with parents who are drunks or druggies. These kids act out; they become criminals and then we call them bad kids. Look at the statistics. Seventy to eighty percent of people in prison have been battered as kids. We have so much crime today in America because of domestic violence.

You can get over it. That's the good news. When I started

dealing with it and my memories came up, I kept asking my therapist, "Are you sure this is worth it?" because all you feel is agitation and pain. I went through weeks when I was on the brink of tears all the time for no reason. But you do get beyond it and break through to the other side. I slip sometimes; I revert to old thinking; but as years go on, I'm developing new habits. I revert less and less often. Having a healthy self-attitude is becoming more the norm, and I reinforce it constantly. Every day I get a little bit better.

Just recently I learned something about my mother that's helped me put my situation in perspective. I was on a talk show promoting my book when a woman called in saying she was my mother's sister. After the show I called her up. We hadn't had any contact over the years, but I remembered her once having babysat me. Something told me we had to get together. When we did, she indicated that there had been a lot of unhappiness in her family—my mother's family. She gave me information indicating that my mother had been molested by her father, probably throughout her childhood. From other family members, I learned that my mother's grandmother also physically abused my mother. I know that my mother hated her grandmother, so much so that she had her middle name legally changed so that it was no longer the same as her grandmother's.

Having this knowledge about my mother explains why there was no possibility that she could have had a happy marriage. She and my dad had six children, but there had to be a lot of anger tied up with just the sexual act itself. During this time nobody went to therapy and nobody talked about these things. I feel pain now when I think of what her life must have been like. She had to live with those memories. I now can understand her unexplainable rage when I would get caught playing doctor as a child. It reflects the issues that she took from her own childhood of having to have sex when she was very young, in a totally awful way. It's great to make those connections. It helps in the healing process. Sex for my mother was her worst nightmare. It had very shameful associations.

Knowing what I now know about my mother has really helped me come to understand her. I don't think my mother was ever able to speak to another living soul about what she'd endured as a child. Now I can better appreciate why she behaved as she did toward me and my brothers.

When I wrote about "Patient Zero," Gaetan Dugas, the guy who knowingly spread AIDS, my first thought was, "He's a jerk, totally narcissistic." Yet here's somebody who was an orphan, adopted by a strict Catholic family in Quebec City where they really knew how to be strict, and I can't help but wonder what happened to him as a kid. Somebody who was that callous to other human beings must have had some terrible darkness in his past. The point I'm trying to make is that the beat goes on—the generational cycle of abuse. At some point somebody's got to break it. The first thing to do is break the silence. Talk about it. Talking through this book is one way of opening up. I broke my cycle through the help of therapy. Now I'm able to feel sorry for my mom because she probably never talked to anybody about this in her whole life; yet it was the driving force of her life. I would be very surprised if during any of her fifty-nine years on this earth she was ever able to confide in another human being about this awful thing that happened to her. So, I've forgiven her. I've been able to make the connection between the abuse she suffered and her abuse of me. There was always this puzzle with this missing piece. Where did this rage come from? When you're a kid you're always going to blame yourself. When I finally got this piece to the puzzle, it made a portrait of her as a human being whom I could forgive. It lifted a huge load.

Because of abuse, I lost my mother, a mother who could have nurtured me and made me feel valued. I'm sorry for that, but I don't dwell on it. I can only learn from past mistakes. By speaking out, by seeking help, I've resolved to leave her legacy of abuse behind.

*Forgive us our trespasses as we
forgive those who trespass
against us.*

THE LORD'S PRAYER

Brenda Clubine

I FIRST HEARD about Brenda Clubine when she was profiled on "20/ 20." The entire program was devoted to the battered women's syndrome. The women featured were all serving time in prison for fighting back against their abusive husbands. I was particularly taken by Brenda's story.

A clip was aired showing Brenda at her original arraignment. There stood this eighty-pound woman with no front teeth, blackened eyes, and a bruised, swollen face. She walked as though she had a limp from all the bones that had been broken. Her husband—six foot four, 250 pounds—was killed by this frail woman who just couldn't take it anymore. Brenda had hit her husband on the head with a bottle of Cold Duck. I thought of the time I'd hit my father with that tennis racket when I just couldn't take it anymore. An inch one way or another and I might have killed him, too. I instantly felt a strange kinship for this woman who was serving her twelfth year of a sixteen-to-life sentence for the murder of her abusive husband.

I got in touch with Brenda at the Frontera State Prison outside of San Diego and arranged a visit.

The abuse Brenda had suffered at her husband's hands wasn't the first she had encountered. She had been sadistically abused by her adoptive mother as a child.

Brenda started a support group for battered women in prison that has become a model for prisons around the country.

At the time of her trial, the law in California allowed that abuse prior to the night of the murder was admissible in court, but only at the judge's discretion. In Brenda's case, that trial judge decided not to admit Brenda's prior abuse into evidence. Though Brenda had filed for divorce, had dozens of police reports concerning her husband's beatings and a warrant for his arrest for felony battery, plus forty-six different complaints filed against him in the last three months before his death, the judge ruled it inadmissible.

Through her work with abused women in prisons, Brenda has gained a louder voice. In 1991, because of her testimony, the California State Legislature made prior abuse mandatory as evidence. Although this law will affect future cases, it won't help Brenda. She is still behind bars serving her sentence.

BRENDA CLUBINE

J was adopted by the Kargs when I was six months old, but I didn't know I wasn't theirs until I started kindergarten. One day one of the kids at school spit at me and told me I was adopted, but I didn't understand. I didn't know what "adopted" meant. I went home very upset. My parents sat me down then and told me I was special, that they'd chosen me. But I never felt special. My adoptive parents never hugged me or told me they loved me the way they told their real children. I felt left out compared to them.

Basically, I became the maid of the family. When I was nine, my mother had a nervous breakdown. I was taken out of school so I could look after everybody. I learned how to cook, clean, and do laundry. I made sure everybody made their beds and did their homework. That went on for a year. When I was ten, I was finally permitted to go back to school, but by then I had missed so much I had to be held back a year.

My mother's abusive behavior toward me started in the third grade. Things went downhill from there. My dad had a tendency to want to hear me out but my mom would blame me; then they would fight over it. She always said everything was my fault. It was just one thing after the other. She'd say, "You little bitch. You're just like your mother. We can take you back." I didn't know who my mother was and I don't believe she ever knew who my mother was, but she used this to intimidate me. When she threatened me like that, I remember thinking, "Take me back to where?" I'd never lived anywhere else. I don't know if I felt hurt as much as I felt she didn't love me.

I remember a particularly bad day back when I was in the sixth grade. I didn't know what I had done wrong, but she hit me so many times with a belt that I was black and blue all over my back and all the way down the backs of my legs. My mother didn't say anything to me; she just kept whooping me.

I was the only one she ever beat. My brothers and sisters never even got grounded. I figured it was my fault; there had to be something wrong with me. I grew up my whole life thinking that she was right and I was doing something wrong.

After one of my first beatings, I didn't dress for physical education at school for two weeks. My P.E. teacher said that she would have to fail me for every day I didn't dress. I still refused to change. Finally the teacher made me undress. When she saw my back and legs, she called the authorities. By the time I got home, an officer had already been to my house. When I walked in my mother said, "Well, if you're going to tell them, I'm going to give you something to tell them about." And I got it again. So I learned not to tell anybody. I did tell the P.E. teacher what my mother did, but the school never followed it up.

Not long after this episode, my mother beat me with an extension cord. It sliced the back of my leg, but by then, I had decided to skip P.E. altogether. There was no point trying to get help; I didn't want to risk another beating. And I didn't want to show my bruises in front of all my classmates. I ended up being truant fifty-two times in one semester. I quickly gained the reputation of being a bad kid.

As a regular punishment, my mother would make me lie face down on the carpet—not on my cheek but with my nose right on the carpet. She wouldn't let me move and I couldn't go to the bathroom. I had to stay there that way for a minimum of four hours. Most of the time it was six. I wasn't allowed to make any noise or speak. I wasn't permitted to move or do anything, not even go to the bathroom. If I wet my pants, I got a whooping.

My mother never apologized for anything she ever did to me. My dad would try to explain her behavior. He'd tell me that she was overly emotional, that she was handling things the best way she knew how. I told my dad that I was afraid she was going to kill me one day, but he never really tried to stop her.

I was thirteen when I left home. Two weeks before I left, I was raped. To this day I don't know who raped me; my assailant was never apprehended. I had been at a mall. My mother had told me to be sure to be home before dark, but inside the mall it looks light even after sunset. I was walking home and this guy pulled his car in front of me. He hopped out, grabbed me, stuck a rag in my mouth, then shoved me in his car. He stuck the rag so far down my throat, I thought I was going to throw up. He told me that if I tried anything, he would kill me. I was terrified. I wet my pants. He had a big knife; it seemed gigantic, like a machete, although I'm sure it wasn't really quite that big. He held the knife at my throat while he took me on a drive. We ended up in some motel in Glendale on Colorado Boulevard. He must have already rented the room. He held my hands above my head with one of his hands; then he raped me several times.

It hurt a lot. I was a virgin. It hurt so much, I decided I never wanted to have sex with anyone.

After it was over, he fell asleep. I didn't even take the time to get my clothes because they were over by his stuff and I was afraid if he woke up, he'd grab me. So I just left. I didn't even grab a blanket.

I ran to the police station. A policeman took off his shirt and gave it to me. He called my parents. My mother came down. When she got there he told her that he wanted her to take me to the hospital to be checked into the rape crisis center. She didn't. They also told her I needed to come in for a pregnancy test in two weeks.

My mother was very cold to me. I was still very upset, but she never once tried to comfort me. She seemed angry at me.

On the way home that night I felt so ashamed and scared. I asked my mother what we would do if I was pregnant. She said, "You'll have the baby and we'll give it to someone in the church." We got into a big argument about this. I said, "What if I don't want to have the baby?" But my mother said that it didn't matter. It wouldn't be my decision to make.

The next day when I left for school, my mother said, "From now on I'm going to give you twenty-five minutes to get home after school. If you're not home and I have to come looking for you, there's going to be trouble." I said okay.

Two weeks after that I got home five minutes past the twenty-five-minute time limit. When I came in through the front door, my mother cold-cocked me—she punched me, knocking me to the ground.

I just snapped. I got up off the ground, grabbed her by the neck and put her up against the French doors and said, "You will never hit me again. This is it. It is over." She said, "If you don't like it here, there's the door." I went upstairs, packed my little backpack and that was it. I got my savings book and I left.

I ended up in Oceanside. I got a job as a waitress. And I got involved with a guy who was twenty-eight. He thought I was nineteen; really I was just fourteen and a half. We dated eleven months before I ever let him touch me. Finally we got married.

Johnny was a chopper pilot in the Air Force. He was sent to Vietnam two weeks after our wedding. I was pregnant. When our daughter was one month old, Johnny came home on a two-week leave. When he left, I was pregnant again. Seven months later he was killed in action.

I felt despondent. I had learned to truly love him. After Johnny died, I met a man at the hospital where I was working. Eight months later we were married, but it was a mistake. Although the marriage only lasted for six weeks, I got pregnant.

I was pregnant when Robert, my third husband, met me. He knew I was pregnant, but he didn't mind at all. He was very protective of me and he was good to my kids. We never argued. He sent me flowers at work, took me to lunch. It was a happy time.

I weighed eighty pounds; he was six foot four and weighed 250 pounds and was a policeman. I saw him as my protector. I felt secure. He could take care of me and my children. We lived together off and on for five years. But once we got married, things started changing.

Robert was very close to his mother, and they had a strange relationship. I don't know how, but she maneuvered her way into living with us. The day before she was to move in with us, I went to pick up Robert at her house. I walked in on them just in time to see Robert slap her across her face. I ran over to her and stood between them. "What are you doing? Are you crazy? Why did you hit your mom?" He grabbed me, picked me off the ground and threw me against the doorjamb. He walked toward me with a look on his face like nobody was there, yelling, "It's none of your business. You need to stay out of it. You can't tell me what to do." Then he started hitting me. I was screaming at him to stop. All the while his mom just sat there. I got away from him and tried to call the police, but he yanked the phone off the wall. The neighbors heard the noise and they called the police. When they pulled up into the driveway, Robert went out to meet them. They shook hands, talked. They were his buddies. He knew all of them from work. After that the police just left. They never even came up to me. I snuck out the back and went home. My mouth and lip were puffed up out past my nose by the time I got there and I could barely move my neck.

Later Robert couldn't have been more apologetic. He said he was sorry a hundred times. I accepted his tears and flowers; then it was just one thing after another. Over the next eleven years he got more and more violent. Many times he dangled me over the edge of a third-floor balcony holding me by my feet, threatening to drop me. He also grabbed me around my neck as if to choke me. He beat me often. Finally, when it got too bad, I left and went into hiding, but even that didn't work. A restraining order did no good and the police did nothing. He tracked me down and showed up at the parking lot of the country club where I worked. He caused a scene, smashing the windshield of my car. Robert said that if I didn't come home to him, the next time it wouldn't be my windshield getting smashed; it would be my head. The president of the country club told me he was sorry, but they couldn't handle my personal problems. I'd have to find another job.

When I still wouldn't go back to Robert, he bribed the manager of the apartment complex where I was living to get my keys. I came home one day and there he was. We argued and he punched me in the face, then dragged me all over the house by my ankles. It ripped

179

the skin off my face. I ended up with three broken ribs. One punctured my lung. He broke my collarbone and tried to stick a knife through my throat, but I grabbed it and it went through my hand.

I left Robert eleven times. It was easier to go back to him than to have him hunt me down. I went back to the house with his mother and my children. But the abuse continued. There weren't any reasons. Anything would set him off. Maybe I wasn't somewhere he wanted me to be, or he saw me talking, or I got a letter that was addressed specifically to me, or I took too long at the grocery store. My husband strip-searched me. I now realize I was just as sick in my own way because I didn't put an end to it; but I didn't realize I could. I was seeing a psychologist who kept telling me that I must be doing something to set him off. My preacher said, "The home is important. You've got to work this out."

In between incidents he would be so apologetic. I'd have this six-foot-four man with tears in his eyes telling me that he loved me and he was really sorry. He never had a good explanation. He'd say it was stress or his mother was pushing him too much, but mostly it was me. If I wouldn't have said something in that tone of voice or if I would have done something that I was specifically supposed to do, it wouldn't have happened. And, like when I was a little girl, I was starting to think that it was me. I was starting to think, if I could just be a better wife, he wouldn't have to hit me.

It was the same reinforcement. My mother told me it was me, my husband's saying it was me, and my second husband said it was me, so you know what? Everybody must be right. It's me. Something's seriously wrong with me. I tried to kill myself twice. I took a lot of pills. The last time was the worst. I took thirty Valiums, thirty Darvons, and six Quaaludes. I woke up two weeks later with tubes and wires all over me. I remember opening my eyes and seeing my physician standing there. I was sorry I wasn't dead because life was hell. Everything was the same and now I was in more pain.

I went back home, but this time when I got out of the hospital, Robert wasn't there; he had moved out. I was relieved he was gone. In the last six months, I filed forty-six different complaints with the police department and a restraining order. Every one of those forty-six times was because of his beating me up, breaking into my house, vandalizing my car, or leaving threatening messages on my answering machine. It would start out nice, "Please call me," but by the end it was, "YOU BITCH I'M GOING TO KILL YOU! PICK UP THE PHONE! I KNOW YOU'RE THERE." He would make nine or ten calls in a matter of an hour.

Finally I filed for divorce. Robert agreed to meet me and sign the divorce papers. I insisted we do it in a public place. Robert agreed to meet me at a Bob's Big Boy.

During dinner he told me he'd left the divorce papers in his motel room. I told him I wasn't going to go to his motel room. I had a bad feeling. But Robert insisted there was nothing to worry about. Stupidly (again) I believed him. Reluctantly I agreed to go back with him. But when we got there, he locked the door behind me, tore up the divorce papers and threw them in my face. He started questioning me about the warrant I'd filed against him for felony battery. Then he asked me to give him my wedding rings. I did, but asked why. "Because without these, they're not going to be able to identify your body." He snapped his finger. "I can kill you that fast and nothing will happen to me."

I was convinced he was going to kill me. I tried to humor him, but the minute he went into the bathroom I took off. I ran down the stairs and drove off. The next thing I knew, he pulled in front of my car and stopped me. Then he carried me back to the motel room. He hit me a couple of times, backhanding me across my face. He started drinking Cold Duck from the bottle. He wanted to rehash the felony warrant again. I told him I didn't know what he was talking about, that I loved him, that he could forget the divorce. I was scared and just wanted to get out of there.

He smacked the back of my head onto the table. Then he smacked my face into the table and broke my front teeth. I tried talking him out of it. I tried to calm him down. I told him I'd give him a backrub, anything so he wouldn't hurt me any more—all this through broken teeth.

He sat on the side of the bed and I started to rub his back. I was so scared. Then I saw his arm go up. I didn't know if he was going to hit me or not, but I saw that bottle of Cold Duck on the floor and without thinking I grabbed it and swung. He grabbed the fat end of it and said, "What are you doing?" I said, "I'm hurting you like you hurt me." Then I grabbed the bottle back with both my hands and swung again. This time I hit him with it. He fell across the bed holding the back of his head. He was moaning. I ran out of the room terrified that when he came to he would come after me and kill me.

When they found him, he had two stab wounds in his back: one in his shoulder blade a sixteenth of an inch deep and one in his shoulder a quarter of an inch deep. I don't remember stabbing him, but I must have because I was the only one who was there. The stabs were superficial. It was the blow to his head that killed him. I was stunned to hear he was dead. I hadn't known I killed him. At the trial I learned that Robert had the thinnest skull of anyone the medical examiner had ever seen. His was only two and a half millimeters thick, when the average human skull is five millimeters thick. Robert's skull shattered where I hit him and his brain hemorrhaged. It took him between sixteen and twenty-two hours to die.

In my trial all prior abuse was ruled inadmissible. I was convicted of second-degree murder and sentenced to sixteen years to life. I felt so misunderstood. I wasn't able to say, "Don't you know what he did to me?"

I'd been behind bars a couple of years when I asked if there was any kind of group or counseling for abuse victims. I was told that one time they had held a battered women's group for two nights, but no one showed up so they never tried to do it again. A couple more years went by. During this time I read everything I could on the subject of abuse. There were so many women in prison for the same thing—women who finally fought back. We needed to be able to talk. So I asked the prison program administrator if *I* could start a group for abused women. She offered me her office, but insisted she be there, too.

In November 1988, I chaired our first meeting, called Convicted Women Against Abuse. That night about ten people showed up. After that, word got out that something good was happening. We now have forty-four members and we talk about our feelings. We all have so much in common. No one had ever listened to any of us before. It was strange hearing these women tell essentially the same story of repeated abuse. Sharing our lives has been very healing. I feel a little better all the time knowing I'm not the only one. I don't feel so alone any more; but it's frightening to think the violence is so pervasive and so little is being done to stop it.

All my life I've been in situations where I am out of control. I have a lot of feelings about that. I get very frustrated realizing I have put myself in one situation after another where I have no control.

Starting my support group has come back to me in many positive ways. Every time I meet with my group and I see how they've grown and how they feel about themselves, I believe, no matter what's happened, I'm here for a reason. I feel one day I'll be free. I can't stay in here forever.

I long to have a normal life and to be with my children again. When you live with someone who's out of control, you get addicted to the behavior. That's why there are abusive relationships, because it becomes normal. As sick as that person is, you get just as sick along with them. That's why I can't answer when someone asks why I didn't leave him. I know right away that they don't understand the syndrome.

I'm fighting ninety percent of the population because most people are unenlightened about this syndrome. Women have to get themselves out of abusive situations before it's too late. If every abused woman could understand that every abusive relationship is potentially fatal, it might be enough to shake her up.

Today I understand—*if he hits you once, he will hit you again!*

Sexual Abuse

No one knows for sure how many victims of sexual abuse there are. There is no accurate system for gathering the statistics. Even if there were, the results would probably not be precise since so many keep it a secret or repress the memories as a coping mechanism. These memories can be triggered by anything, from a seemingly insignificant event to a major trauma, and those who choose to repress such memories of abuse often suffer ramifications despite their best efforts to the contrary.

The victim who uses repression as protection from the hurt is nonetheless tormented by unexplained feelings of worthlessness, shame, unhappiness, depression, sexual repulsion, and confusion. In extreme situations, split personalities can also result.

Sexual abuse is any unwanted touching. When a child cannot prevent or control objectionable touching or fondling of his or her own body, that child is victimized and that is abuse.

"Sexually abusive acts range from voyeurism and exhibitionism to masturbation, to rape and sodomy, to bestiality, to ritualized torture in cults. Incest may or may not include penetration, may or may not be violent. It may happen only once or continue for decades. It usually exists in secret, but not always," writes Heidi Vanderbilt in *Lears*.

Incest is abuse of a child by a relative or any person placed in a position of trust and authority over a child. It is the ultimate violation because the child involved relies upon the abuser for help and protection. Who can the child turn to if not to those who are supposed to take care of them?

Small children understand very little about sex. They trust that whatever happens at the hands of those in charge of them is right. So, the sexual abuser takes advantage of both his position of trust and the child's innocence.

Sexual abusers often force children to keep the secret through threats. Dan Sexton's abuser said, "If you tell, I will do this to one of your brothers or sisters, or I will tell your friends, or I will cut the brakes on your parents' car."

In Cheryl Crane's case, her mother's third husband threatened to send her away, never to see her mother again.

Dr. William Rader of the Rader Institute says: "The people you trust more than anyone in the whole world are your parents. They are there to protect you. So if trust is violated in the safest place in the world with the people who are supposed to protect you, how can you ever trust any human being again? When this happens to a little child, it's the ultimate loss of control. Children do not have any defense mechanisms; therefore, they don't know how to deal with it. They also believe that if this happened in their own home, then their home is the way life is going to be.

"One child of abuse recently wrote a letter to her father saying, 'Daddy, you took everything from me. You took my dignity, you took my soul, you took my ability to see life as beautiful, you gave me incredible anxiety about the whole world, you stripped everything from me. You came in the middle of the night and every night I would wait for you to come. Even if you didn't come, you would take that night away because of my fear that you would. And I remember, Daddy, so clearly, I remember the sperm going down my little throat.' Do you know what was the next thing she said in the letter? She said, 'I love you, Daddy. I went to church and I prayed for you, Daddy.' That's the whole gist right there. The most important thing in someone's life is parental love. It is more important than anything. It is so important, it's like breath, life itself. If you don't have that, you feel you might as well die. Therefore, whatever your parent does is right and you are wrong. You will always make that choice because otherwise, if your parents are really doing this bad thing to you, then life is over. So you will make yourself guilty and you will make yourself responsible for what's going on. The sperm going down her throat is the horror and right behind that is, 'I love you, Daddy, and I pray for you at church, Daddy.' In other words, 'It is my fault, Daddy.' The child believes it is his or her fault. The father reinforces that it is her fault by telling her that it is and that she is dirty and she is shameful. Remember, the parental figure is saying this, so she's going to believe it because she's a child and she doesn't have defense mechanisms. It is a major confusion. Now put on top of this that sexuality is physical. Sometimes it feels good and sometimes she has an orgasm, but she doesn't know what it is."

Richard Berendzen relates this same confusion. He loathed the abuse, but his confusion lay in the fact that it also felt good.

Dr. Rader says: "Children can feel and have good feelings. It's not the same kind of orgasm that an adult will have, but something happens. So they're further convinced that the victimizer is correct. If they really weren't bad and wrong, how could they possibly feel good?

"Often a victim will never identify who his abuser is because in his mind it is his fault. If it wasn't his fault, why did he feel good as a child when it happened? He becomes totally convinced he is responsible. The abuser also says to the child, 'No matter where you go, no matter where you are, I can see you and I will know if you tell anybody about this; and if you do, I will punish you or I will kill you.' The child believes all this. So in the safest place in the world with the person or persons they love and trust the most—the parents—this occurs. Also, a great deal of the time the mother is aware of it. If the child, at some level, realizes this (by the time he or she gets to be an adult), initially the anger is toward the father but then it moves to Mom. 'Where were you? Why didn't you take care of me? Why didn't you protect me?' "

Carol Trenery, Director of Sahuaro Vista Ranch, a women's treatment center in Tucson, Arizona, says: "Women have often stood by and watched their children being beaten or sexually violated and not really had a sense that they could do anything about it. They dealt with it by pretending it wasn't happening. That's why there are a lot of people angry with their mothers today, because some of them know their mothers were aware of what was going on. 'Why didn't you help me?' "

Difficult as it is for girls to talk about their abuse, it is even harder for boys. For a boy to report that he was abused, he must admit weakness and victimization. Dr. Rader says: "If a boy is molested by a male, he will fear that this has made him homosexual. He believes he must be homosexual and then he might spend time being homosexual feeling it's bad, dirty, and wrong. The greater percentage of homosexuals know they are homosexuals at an early age. Homosexuality is a normal state for them. But there are some who go this direction because of incest and feel that's what they should be; that that is what they deserve. By acting out homosexuality, these people treat sex the way addicts do: there's no feeling in conjunction with the sex. And the sex is furtive—it's here, there, everywhere, no real intimacy. The act makes them feel degraded, but it takes the pain away and makes them feel okay for the moment."

Carol Trenery says that of the women who come in for addictions treatment at her center, over ninety percent have been sexually violated through incest, molestation by a friend, rape, date rape: a variety of ways, quite often more than one. If such abuse started early in the victim's life, a pattern of victimization is established. Such people get themselves in situations where they continue to be victims. Not that they are asking for it, but it's a pattern into which they do drift.

"It starts when they are so young they don't know that they can say no. Quite often it's the only kind of attention they ever got from a family member. A lot of the violation is by women to women or women to girls. It could be a mother violating a daughter or an aunt violating a niece. These women come from a variety of backgrounds and addictions; we don't sort them out. Alcoholism doesn't go over here and food over there.

"One woman came to us who had had a back injury for several years. That became the basis from which she carried her pain. In therapy she began to get in touch with herself and what had happened to her in her life. Memories began to return and she remembered having been molested. The more memories that surfaced, the more back pain she felt. The pain expanded with her recollections at this time; it became generalized throughout her body. She needed a cane to get around. She looked like an old woman, but she was only thirty-five years old. She looked and moved like a sixty-year-old, a fifty-five-year-old at least. She was tired; her children had to take care of her. She could hardly even do housework. For all intents and purposes, she had become an invalid. Through therapy she started to get in touch with all the guilt and shame. The molestation that she first remembered was by a priest. A lot of shame went along with the fact that the man who had molested her was a clergyman. This person was supposed to have been a man of God yet he had imposed himself upon her. The episode killed whatever chances for spiritual development she may have had. As she went through life, she was violated by other men. As she began to work through her painful past, she began to make nearly daily improvements. All her emotional trauma had translated into physical pain. As she was able to deal with it and move through the emotional pain, the physical pain started to lift. By the time she finished treatment, her recovery was one of the most astonishing I've ever seen. The years had fallen away. She was standing taller, she was moving without the use of a cane."

It is not unusual for victims of sexual abuse to grow up with sexual problems. Some can't touch or be touched. Traci Lords was repulsed by sex and couldn't stand the thought of anyone touching her because of the shame and guilt she felt from her father's *verbal* sexual abuse. Then she reversed herself completely, acting out by become wildly promiscuous in adult films.

According to Marti Heuer, an adolescent drug and alcohol counselor and author of *Happy Daze:* "Underneath the obnoxious behavior is an extremely hurt child who has put up emotional barriers so she will not get hurt any more by adults. Sexually abused children feel they've been lied to and no one has taken the time to understand what's going on inside of them. Usually that child starts to become comfortable with negative attention instead of positive attention. It's a form of being noticed and a way of getting their anger out. You know, 'Go ahead and hit me. You think I'm going to be a slut or a whore, fine; that's exactly what I'm going to be, and I'm going to be great at it.' Underneath they desperately need somebody to get past all the baloney. They desperately want someone to get down to how they feel and what's happening to them. At the same time they'll fight that very effort because they are scared.

"A basic sense of loyalty runs very deep in kids, even ones who've been abused. I've seen children who were physically abused by a parent, but when they are in court and asked, 'Do you want to go back?' they'll say yes. Blood is thicker than water. There is a biological bond.

"In abusive families there can be overt incest and/or covert incest. Some girls in treatment may not be able to describe any tangible incest, but their feelings are the same as an incest victim. There has not been a genital contact made with their dad or step-dad, but there's been an emotional and verbal bond of some kind that has moved her inappropriately into the wife's role in some way. Emotionally she might be looked upon to support her dad. A kind of triangulation can go on in which the father will come to the daughter and say, 'Your mom doesn't understand me at all. I need you to talk to me and understand me.' The girl will try to do that with her dad and the mother will say, 'Your dad is a son-of-a-bitch.' The child is in the triangle and she needs to be loved and accepted by both. She doesn't know how to get out of it."

Some victims of extreme sexual abuse are unable to feel physical pain, so they self-mutilate. Debby Goodman would cut herself with a knife, making deep gashes in her arms. "It's like I wanted to get the dirty part to ooze out. I wanted to relieve the pressure and I also felt I deserved to desecrate my body. It was almost as though I blamed my own body as the cause of my problems." Debby is also plagued by physical illnesses: a bad back, severe anxiety attacks, and stomach problems.

Carol Trenery says: "Women take on physical illnesses more than men as a way of coping. It's a way to deal with the pain. Because they can't deal with it acceptably on an emotional level, they can get people to talk to them about their ulcers or their headaches or back pains. If you talk to different people, some will use terms like, 'I just can't get her off my back. My mom's always on my back.' Those people will complain a lot about back pains. If you watch people who stuff their feelings as they get angry, you'll see them swallow a lot. They may have lots of stomach problems, internal problems. People who refer to someone else as a real pain in the ass may end up with colon cancer. So, it's all about where you hold onto that. Our subconscious speaks the truth more than we realize. As you begin to find out what the pain is, the memories return."

Abuse survivors are treated for PTSD, post-traumatic stress disorder. Survivors of abuse live with constant and sometimes crippling anxiety. The symptoms of PTSD are demonstrated by some returning Vietnam War veterans and victims of torture. They suffer nightmares, flashbacks, amnesia, unexplained fear and anger, and severe anxiety. Cheryl Crane often speaks of "leaving her body" during the abuse by her mother's third husband. It was a way to disassociate herself from the horror of the act. She just "wasn't there." Many victims continue to disassociate for decades after the abuse ends. The longer the duration, the more severe the trauma, the more likely a victim will develop PTSD.

Victims can also cope by developing multiple-personality disorders. When the abuse suffered is violent and sadistic, as in the case of Debby Goodman, the mind falls apart. She dealt with this by having a conscious life and an unconscious life. By day she had a relatively normal routine; by night she was victimized by cult rituals, including multiple rape and unimaginable acts of violence. At night she became her "other self." The two personalities did not know each other. In other cases each violent assault is handled by one or more personalities. Some "selves" hold pain, others grief, others rage.

A sexually abused child or adult has great difficulty with trust. A patient of Dr. Rader tells that at age five her father raped her. "Yet she was convinced (at age twenty-eight) that it was she who had seduced her father. She was convinced this was the issue. She was afraid to be intimate with someone because that person would come close to her awful truth. In addition, there is that basic Pavlovian conditioning going on. After so much betrayal by the abuser through sexual intimacy, it's hard for the victim to trust anyone with whom she is sexually intimate. The victim thinks, 'My father did this, so how do I know you're not going to stab me in the middle of lovemaking?' Of course, this is never discussed. This is not even thought about; and, of course, they'll be faking orgasms because an orgasm might trigger the early orgasms or the early feelings of good. So how can they fully allow themselves to be vulnerable ever again?

"A father has the capacity to trigger the baby in you in a way that no one else can, not even your husband. The victim still believes that at some level, her father has some kind of power over her and can carry out the kinds of threats he made when she was a child. That belief may have nothing to do with reality." Witness Marie Williams, who still fears her father even though he is now in jail. She is convinced he will kill her when he gets out.

"Often those who were abused abuse, but not always. When they do abuse, it's usually because they're locked in a pattern; they treat their children the way they themselves were treated. It's scary because it's the last thing in the world they say they're going to do. It's the same thing as children of alcoholics who say, 'I'm never going to drink.' A lot of 'normal people' say, 'I'll never do what Mom or Dad does. I'll never be like them,' and then they find themselves repeating it. This is what is normal for them. They repeat that pattern. The statistics say they will do that unless they get the information. Once they start acting out negatively, they really believe they're bad and horrible. Look at the bully at school. However it starts, once he's the bully, everybody thinks he's the bully and then he will meet their expectations. It's the same with the hero. How does somebody get to be a hero? Everybody sees him as the hero, so he acts like a hero. Go to the nursery at a hospital and look at the newborn babies. Who are the bad ones, the good ones, the obscene phone callers? They're all just pure little kids. Where they are going to fall on the scale of good to bad is determined by what kind of input they get."

"The one thing a child learns from sexual abuse is how to be abused," says Dr. Summit in Heidi Vanderbilt's article on incest, in the February 1992 issue of *Lear's*. "Sexually abused children teach themselves to endure assault. Instead of learning to protect themselves, they learn they can't protect themselves. Someone who has never been abused can say, 'No,' walk or run away, can scream and fight. The incest victim often doesn't know what to do except wait for the danger to be over."

Dr. Rader says: "Incest is such a horrendous act because it's with a child and the confusion is incredible. Many incest victims feel that this is love. A lot of times males and females become promiscuous because this is the only way they feel they are going to get love; to them, this is what love is about. If real intimacy comes along, they are going to run. If there are 500 men in the room and 499 of them will give them real intimacy and one will not, that's the one the incest survivor will choose. I had a woman I treated when I was doing private therapy who in one year had dated and slept with over 200 men. All were between the ages of thirty-five and forty-two, which was the age of her father at the time of her incest. All were married. They were cold and were certainly not committed to her or concerned with her welfare. She thought the whole world consisted of these kinds of men because she always found them. It was incredible. It became a self-fulfilling prophecy. If an incest survivor like this woman met someone who was genuinely concerned about her, someone who really cared, chances are she would shy away from him. She wouldn't want to let anyone get that close to her issues because she wouldn't feel she deserved it."

We tend to think we will recognize perpetrators of a crime as horrendous as sexual abuse. We imagine they have beady eyes and horns growing from their heads. Yet, as you read the following stories, you will find that this is not the case. Most of the contributors to this book were molested by parents or trusted family friends. Therein lies the shock and confusion. The perpetrator is almost always someone the child trusts. How can that person ever trust anyone again? Sexual abuse carries with it lifelong damage.

Sexually abused children almost all suffer similar symptoms, chiefly damaged self-esteem, which leads to self-destructive behavior. They almost all feel worthless and unlovable. They describe an emptiness or an internal deadness.

When such children grow up, they carry feelings of guilt and inadequacy which makes it very difficult for them to develop a positive sense of self. Some abused children choose suicide when the pain of their past overwhelms them.

Marti Heuer says: "Children have rights, but we never teach them their basic rights as persons in this world. They have the right to change their minds. They have the right not to have people touch them in ways they don't want to be touched. They have the right to talk to someone they can trust about how they feel inside. They have the right to their feelings."

Dr. Rader says: "Sexual abuse doesn't just happen. There are warning signs. To the outside world the father seems like a real nice guy; but when you check inside his home, you find that before he incestuously molested his daughter, he was doing a lot of things. He was verbally abusive, he was impatient and controlling or feeling hen-pecked. He was already picking on the child. There are a lot of signs which indicate sexual abuse may follow. It's important to remember that what the father is doing to that child is not about sex, which is confusing because a penis and a vagina are involved, or a mouth, whatever, but it's not sex. It's about control. I think society has finally learned that rape is about control. It's the same thing here. For the abuser, sexual abuse is about feeling powerful when he or she really feels he or she isn't powerful. For these people, dealing with equals in age, intellect, or physical ability can be very threatening, but with a little child, the abuser feels powerful. If we could train ourselves as a society to look for the warning signs, we might go a long way toward curbing the sexual abuse of children."

Many adults who were sexually abused as children feel there is no real meaning to life. They feel beaten down; life is to be endured. They have no sense of who they are, no sense of a right to define themselves. Only after they begin to acknowledge their illtreatment and understand and accept that it wasn't their fault can they begin to turn their lives around. Finally, they own the right to define who they want to be.

Abuse is defined as trauma to one's person.
That abuse affects every single way
a child then views himself and
affects every relationship, be it
personal or sexual, he may then have.
The longer the abuse took place, the more severe the
degree of violence involved,
and most importantly, the closer
the relationship between the perpetrator
and the victim, the more dramatically
the impact of the sexual abuse is compounded.

SIGNE TIMME, L.C.S.W.
Coordinator of
Adult Survivors of
Sexual Abuse Program

B. J. Thomas

Raindrops keep fallin' on my head
But that doesn't mean my eyes
Will soon be turning red
Cryin's not for me
I'm never gonna stop the rain
By complaining
Because I'm free
Nothin's worryin' me . . .

BACK IN 1965 *when this song was the mega-hit theme to the movie*
Butch Cassidy and the Sundance Kid, *B. J. Thomas had no idea of*
the impact these lyrics would eventually have on his life. At that time
he was just singing his songs, enjoying the fame and fortune stardom
can bring. After all, this is what he wanted: to be a country and western
singing star and to have the money and fame that accompanied it.
Maybe he could finally get the approval he so desperately wanted from
his abusive, alcoholic father. Maybe he could finally purge himself of
the shame he carried as a child sexually abused at the hands of a
relative.

His dad idolized Hank Williams, so B. J. believed that if he
achieved the same kind of status, he could break through the barriers
that kept his father at a distance all his life. But stardom and five
Grammys couldn't bridge that gap.

B. J. suffered under the dual curse of sexual abuse and alcoholism.

He turned to alcohol early to fill the emptiness; and the money that accompanied his newfound fame made drugs easily accessible. The drugs and drink took his pain away—just as they had for his father and his father's father before him.

B. J.'s meteoric rise shifted into reverse. The big wave he was riding quickly crashed on the shore through his dual addictions. B. J. started appearing on stage and on TV stoned. He rambled, he didn't make sense, and the public got turned off. It wasn't until he overdosed that he realized his secret past was driving him into the grave. He sought treatment and his life took a distinct turn upward. In the process he was finally able to see his childhood and the relationship he couldn't have with his father as his opportunity, not a determining factor.

B. J. THOMAS

*W*HEN you're a kid, there is no such thing as sexual abuse. When you're a kid you don't say, "God, one of my relatives is sexually abusing me." You say to yourself, "He is putting his penis in my mouth, and there's something wrong with that." As a kid, I never made this relative out to be wrong. I just thought I was not worth a damn; that this was all I was good for. I made myself wrong. I didn't chalk any of my feelings up to what my relative did to me. I just decided I wasn't worth anything. I developed an act to compensate—being different. I had long hair. It was halfway down to my waist when I was eleven, and this was back in 1952. I wouldn't cut my hair no matter what. I just had to be different. That was my method of survival.

I'm sure some sexually abusive things happened when I was an infant, but most of what I actually remember happened when I was very young. By the time I was in the second or third grade, the abuse had stopped.

Now, I didn't remember being abused this way until I went through a five-day dysfunctional family workshop when I was forty-three years old. On the second day of that week, it came back to me. Up until then, I'd blocked it out. And I mean completely.

At first I was in a rage. How could my relative have been so despicable? How could he have treated me this way? But gradually I began to reach a place where I could see that he did what he did out of his own dysfunction.

From what I understand now, abused kids can take this behavior to mean, "This is how you're loving me." They equate sexual abuse with love. Then when they've grown, they show their love this same way. Now I don't know for sure if the relative who abused me was sexually abused, but I have good reasons to believe he was. I know my father was by his father. These things get handed down, one generation to another, like some awful legacy. Today I admire my father, because even though he physically and verbally abused me throughout my childhood, he must have had to work really hard not to act out sexually with me.

I guess I'm lucky. I repressed the abuse; didn't remember one speck of it. It was just too painful. So I didn't wind up passing it along to my kids. But that doesn't mean I didn't suffer the consequences any less. And now that I do remember, I have a better handle on what's happened to me in the years since.

One thing I couldn't block out is my father's drinking. It's what I remember about him most. He died at the age of fifty-two. They said it was a heart attack, but his death was absolutely drinking-related. If he hadn't died suddenly like that, he would have died slowly. The process had already started. He had such severe brain damage from the alcohol abuse, he was already in the beginning stages of outright insanity. So it's almost like his heart attack was a blessing.

When I look at pictures of my dad, I find it strange that one day I'll be older than him. Every time I look in the mirror it's him I see; we look that much alike. If there'd ever been a chance I'd escape his influence, good and bad, that chance flew out the window with heredity. I'm what you call his spitting image.

Everybody was on my dad's case to quit drinking for as long as I could remember. I think the more people tried to change him, the more they pushed him toward it. Not that he didn't want to quit. He tried lots of times. Back then, no one had any concept that it was a disease. They made my dad out to be weak. Either that, or he didn't love us.

He'd have periods when he'd try to quit. He'd stop for three months at a time. Sometimes he'd go as long as a year. He'd announce he was going on the wagon. One time we even got him down to church, where he accepted Jesus and all that holy roller stuff. He tried all kinds of ways to stay sober, but nothing worked for long. He was never able to get a handle on it. He'd say, "Son, some people love certain foods. I truly love the taste of alcohol."

He would get up at four-thirty or five in the morning and have a six-pack before he went to work. When he was in his best shape, he was about six foot two and weighed about 180 or 185 pounds. But when he hit his early forties he went downhill really fast. He suffered a deterioration of both his muscles and his memory. It was scary to see.

When I was a little guy and my friends were around, I was embarrassed. My friends would say, "God, your dad's funny." And I'd think, "He's not funny; the son-of-a-bitch is drunk." I could never be sure what he would do if I brought a friend over. He might pass out in a chair. He might piss in his pants. In the end, I just never invited anyone over.

I was definitely afraid of my dad, too. All he'd have to do is look at me and say, "Son, when I get home today, if you haven't mowed this lawn, I'm gonna blank, blank, blank," as in "I'm gonna beat the shit outta you, you little bastard." He would scare me. I'd be trembling; my chest would be vibrating like an earthquake. But as soon as he got out the door, there was no fuckin' way I was gonna mow anything. He'd be gone for three or four days, and I wasn't gonna mow shit. Besides, eventually he was gonna get drunk and forget everything he said anyway. To keep us from gettin' beat to death, my mother would mow the lawn. I got to the point where I was just as abusive toward my mother as he was. That's what I was taught to do. I wasn't very supportive of her in a lot of ways. If I had mowed the lawn, he wouldn't have been happy anyway. If I left two blades of grass, it wouldn't be right.

Christmas was probably the worst of all. He would drink more than usual and get real depressed. Then he'd spend all his money. We never had a real Christmas. There were never piles of gifts like you might expect as a kid. Every year I'd get excited. I'd think: "This year's going to be different. This year he's not going to drink." My mother would start on him as early as September. She'd say, "Vernon, this year we've got to do something for the boys."

Somehow, I think her pressing him only made his drinking worse.

As far back as I can remember, my dad was a huge fan of Hank Williams, Ernest Tubbs, and all those old hard-drinkin' country singers. He introduced me to their music; and anytime he was usin' the alcohol, that country music was blarin'. When I look back on it, I realize he could have been a country entertainer himself. He had a great voice and loved to sing, but he had no self-esteem and nothin' within himself to motivate him. Basically I had an extremely hard time communicating with him. There never was a show of affection. I couldn't hug him or kiss him or talk with him in any intimate way. But when I saw how he loved the music, I knew that that could be a way to communicate.

I got to where I could sing those songs, and that would make him happy; but he wouldn't tell me I was good. My dad never really acted like he took a lot of satisfaction or pride in me until I had had four or five million records sold and I became fairly famous. That's when he really took pride in me. I'd be on the road all year and would come home for Christmas or Thanksgiving and I'd find out that he'd been calling the radio station and was on their backs every day to play my records. But he wouldn't tell me that.

When I was a kid, I'd say, "I'm never gonna be like my dad." And then I turned out just like him. And I'm not just talking about looks.

I started drinkin' when I was thirteen or fourteen years old. I started using drugs when I was fifteen. I was on the same track as him. I was gonna die young. I'd sworn I'd never drink, but as soon as I had my first one, I said, "God, this is great." See, I thought of myself as no good. I had to find a way to hide that feeling because if I was no good, I just couldn't survive. So I bought into the same racket as my dad. I even got the same reaction out of my mom. I'd get drunk. When I came home, I'd cuss her up and go crazy. Sure enough, she focused on me totally. She'd hold me and rock me and ask, "Son, what's wrong?" So first the drink made me feel better and then my mom followed by showering so much attention on me.

But it cost me. Drinkin' cost me my health and happiness. And as long as I was into this routine, I was never going to be able to love myself or anybody else. I think the most important thing I lost throughout the whole ordeal was my own true self-expression. And that's exactly what my dad did. I became a carbon copy of him.

I was twenty-six when I married Gloria. She was seventeen. We've been together ever since, which will be twenty-two years this year. We've had some rough times. Up until about a year and a half ago, we'd pass each other in the house saying things like, "I hate you, you son-of-a-bitch." That's about all we had to say to one another.

Gloria came from a dysfunctional past, too. I think her childhood was even worse than mine. When I married her, I was already a full-blown alcoholic. She had some involvement with alcohol and drugs, but it was nowhere near the extent of my involvement.

For a period of about ten years, I would come very close to death on a regular basis, maybe two or three times a month. I'd con some doctor into giving me a prescription for one hundred Placidyls. I know I would have died almost any week if it hadn't been for Gloria bein' there, rollin' me over, feeding me, puttin' coffee in me, or throwin' those pills away. Once I OD'ed in Hawaii. I was over there doin' some one-nighters, and I actually died on an airplane trip from the Big Island to Kaui. When they took me off the plane, my fingernails and lips were black. They hooked me up to whatever it is they hook people like that up to. I woke up a week later.

I had many situations like that. I don't know why I didn't die. I was absolutely tryin' to kill myself. The pain came from not believin' I was worth anything. There was only one way to go: kill myself. I'd get right to the edge and throw down a dozen amphetamines, saying, "Oh, the hell with it; let's do it." The success I had meant nothin'; and yet as a young man I'd always thought if I could make it in show business, I would have everything. Then I thought if I could have this first hit record; then if I could get that million dollars in the bank; then if I could get me that Mercedes, then I could be happy. But when I got it, it meant absolutely nothin'. It didn't deliver me or save me; so I felt like, "Well, hell, what the fuck else is there? This is Hank Williams time, so let's go."

I didn't really make a commitment to be a contributing human being until February of 1986. That's when I was involved in a five-day dysfunctional family workshop conducted by Terry Kellogg at the Hazelden rehab center in Minneapolis, Minnesota. It wasn't until I got there and saw all the bullshit for what it was that I made the commitment to be clean and sober.

I can't say what opened my eyes exactly, but all of a sudden, I just got it. It was my interpretation of events that kept me locked up. As long as I believed I wasn't worth anything, which the way I was treated as a child led me to believe, I'd continue to feel worthless. Okay. So I didn't learn self-esteem from my dad. But maybe I could gain it another way. One thing was for sure: I wasn't going to get it if I was to keep drinking and drugging. Booze and pills may have numbed the pain for a while, but they weren't working any more. If anything, they were just pushing me deeper, making me think less and less of myself. So I just had to change my ways.

It was only after I made a decision to get sober that I remembered how I'd been abused when I was small. They say God doesn't give you any more than you can handle at any one time. I think that's true. I don't think I could have dealt with these memories a day sooner than I remembered them. I would have continued to block them out. Or I would have gotten drunk over them. But remembering them when I did, I was able to put them in perspective. I know that my dad's dad treated him much the way my father treated me. My grandfather was a drinker, too. I knew my dad was afraid of him. He'd say great things about him, but no matter how full of praise his stories started out, they'd always wind down to what a son-of-a-bitch my grandfather was. Heck, my grandfather probably had a son-of-a-bitch for a father, too. This thing just keeps going. But I guess you get the picture.

I'm not a religious person, but my turnaround did keep on track through a born-again experience. Gloria and I turned our lives over to Jesus. I imagine if we were in Turkey, we would have turned them over to Mohammed. But we're here, so Jesus was the ticket for us. That was a big step for me; it was the start of developing a spiritual side. I'm still not a religious person. I have too many bad memories of organized religion to put much stock in it. But I've grown in a very spiritual direction.

I may have gotten sober through some twelve-step work, but I feel I'm staying sober through the love of my family. I made a commitment to Gloria back when I was twenty-six. Today I'm living that commitment on a daily basis. We went through some rough times, both as kids and together. As if our childhoods weren't enough hell, we had to put each other through more of it. But we're not doing that anymore. We've made a commitment for life. To me that's what it's all about. I want to count for somethin'. Man, when you've got that kind of feelin', you can't beat it. I'm not some noble dude; I'm just some guy who's got three kids, a marriage, and can sing a little bit. But I'm gonna try to do it one hundred percent, truly to myself. That's what I'm about; that's what I'd like to do till I die. That's what keeps me goin'.

As simple as "Raindrops Keep Fallin' on My Head" seems, there's a truism in it. It had an impact, and that's what I'm about now. I'm not gonna write Beethoven's Fifth, but I feel the best is yet to come. I've got some texture now; I've been through a lot. I've lived, I've loved, I've died, I've cried, I've felt, I feel, I have my priorities in order. I know the best B. J. is about to emerge and I feel empowered with these feelin's.

*I learned I'm not as
bad as I thought I was.*

MADONNA

Traci Lords

TRACI LORDS IS WISE *beyond her years. It's hard to believe she's only twenty-three. She was sexually abused covertly by her violent, physically abusive father. Although he never hit her or touched her sexually, his constant angry badgering and accusations of promiscuity, coupled with her early development, made her ashamed and angry. Her father always called her a tramp and a whore. Eventually, that's how she came to see herself. As a teenager, she starred illegally in countless pornographic films, eventually coming to national attention because she was underage.*

But the Traci Lords you may think you know is very different from the Traci Lords of today. She's happily married and looking forward to starting a family of her own. She's one of the only people ever to cross over from adult films to legitimate feature films. Recently she starred in John Waters's acclaimed film Cry-Baby.

At first, Traci was reluctant to contribute to this book. She wants to leave her past behind. She does not want to be forever known as "Traci Lords, the former teen porn queen." And she has also become an advocate for children's rights and works closely with Children of the Night, an LA–based organization dedicated to helping teenage prostitutes and drug addicts get off the streets.

Through her work, she has come to realize that breaking the silence is the first step in fighting childhood abuse. And so, in the end, she decided to participate.

TRACI LORDS

MY father's father, my grandfather, drank and he was very strict and very abusive to my grandmother. He used to slap her and beat her all the time. They came from the Ukraine, and I think that was something from the "old country" that they never got over. They believed that was acceptable behavior. It was that whole ownership thing. You know, if your husband wants to have sex with you, and you're not interested—too bad. You lie there and say nothing. To me, it is everything a 90s woman is not.

My father was a very, very possessive alcoholic and very jealous. My mother was eighteen when they married and very beautiful. He was so insecure and guilt-ridden, he thought she must be doing the things he fantasized doing with other women. I'm the second oldest of four girls, all born only a year apart. My mother had these four small children and my father was convinced that somewhere in between she must have a lover. He was drunk twenty-four hours a day. I grew up hiding in closets, under the bed, holding hands with my sisters, hoping that our father would pass out so it would be quiet again.

He was never violent with us, but he was very violent with my mother. He beat her up a lot. One time, he beat her so badly, she had stitches all over her face. It really scared us. My sisters and I would always hide under the table—we had a long tablecloth that almost dragged on the floor. We would hold our breath and cover our ears like we were swimming in a pool. Or we'd hold hands and

213

sing little songs and hope he would stop. We would always try to stop him from hitting my mother, and he would throw us outside and lock the door so we couldn't get in the house. We hated him for hurting her, and we felt sorry for her; but we thought it was normal behavior.

Growing up, my sisters and I thought if we were better daughters, my father wouldn't drink. But no matter how hard we tried to be perfect, no matter how well we behaved, he always came home drunk.

The thing I most remember feeling about my father is fear. He was always so strange about everything—especially sex. My father's biggest problem became my problem when I started to develop physically. I matured really early and was this "Lolita" at ten. My father couldn't deal with the fact that I wore size B bras when I was ten years old. I think seeing us becoming women really scared him and he dealt with it in the wrong way. He always lectured us about sex, "You can't do this and you can't do that." Before I ever thought about sex, it was crammed down my throat. I grew up so early, physically; I was tortured by it and I was ashamed of it. My father thought that since I looked that way, I must be acting out these teenage fantasies—hormones must be raging. He was always accusing me. He would get drunk, see me and my older sister, and accuse us of making out with boys or ask me if I let anyone down my pants. It was so horrible. I was constantly being accused of being a whore. By the time I was ten, I had heard that so many times, and that was before I ever had sex with anyone. So sex was a disgusting thing.

I was always told I was a bad girl because of the way I looked. At school, I got it from the boys, too, yet I was totally innocent; I was a virgin. I'd never even kissed a boy. I didn't kiss anyone until I was thirteen. But they were always coming up to me and pulling my bra strap because I was the only girl in school who had one. It was so humiliating.

By the time I was age twelve, I was completely confused and in a shell. I was shy and scared of the entire world because of the emotional torture. I would just sit there and be quiet, hoping no one would notice me or say anything to me, hoping that they might leave me alone that day. I was incredibly introverted, self-conscious, and scared.

When I was about fourteen, my parents divorced and my mother, my sisters, and I moved to California. I wanted my mother to have a better life, so I was very active in her moving. California was the place I wanted to go. It was Marilyn Monroe's home town, it was movie stars and everything I wanted: palm trees, fame and fortune, and all of that. When I was a little girl, I was always hiding in the closet trying on my mother's clothes and dreaming of being a movie star. It was my biggest fantasy.

At first, I was miserable in California. I hated it. It was complete culture shock. I started hanging out with the wrong people. The kids were so fast there. Before I knew it, I was playing with drugs and doing different things. Initially, it was grass; then it was uppers, and downers, and Quaaludes, and speed; then it was crack, acid, everything imaginable.

I was terribly unhappy at home. My mother was going to school for eight hours, then working for eight hours, so she was never home. She was building a future for herself by going to school and getting her master's degree. We were latchkey kids, basically raising ourselves. That's nothing I hold against my mother today. She was trying to keep a roof over our heads. But because of how hard she had to work, she didn't have the time to be there and say, "How are you?" or notice that we weren't fine. I definitely was the most un-fine of all.

I became this incredibly angry, angry girl. I was so pissed off at the entire world because I felt like my father never supported us. We were always so poor. I was always made fun of in school because of the way I dressed. I didn't have any money. I didn't have anything. The boys always thought I was a cheap girl from the wrong side of the tracks, yet I was still a virgin.

From the time I was ten, I was told I was a slut. After you've heard it so many times, you start thinking, "Well, I'm being accused of these things; how come I don't just go and do it? What's the difference?" I had no self-esteem whatsoever. I had no respect for myself. Then, finally, when I was almost fifteen, I met a boy that I really liked. He was pushing the same things down my throat, "I want to have sex. I want to have sex." So we had sex and I ended up getting pregnant. That was a real traumatic thing for me. All I could hear in my mind was my father saying, "You play, you're going to pay." And I thought, "The world is like this and I am a bad person. He's right." From there I went completely insane. I really lost my mind. I started doing every drug imaginable. For a while, I couldn't stand men at all. I didn't want to be looked at. I didn't want to be touched. I didn't want to be anything.

I ran away to Hollywood that same year. I started hanging out with older people and doing drugs. Then this older man took me to a modeling agency and they signed me up. He told me he would make me a beautiful model, put me on the cover of magazines; but I ended up in sleazy magazines with my clothes half off, drugged out of my mind; I barely remember any of it.

From there, it was one movie set after another. Before I knew it, three years had passed. I was eighteen years old. I was strung out on drugs. I don't know how many videos I had in the stores. I don't know how many men I had slept with—or women. Three years of my life had passed and nobody cared. The entire time, I was hoping the police would come save me or my mother would find me or somebody would make everything all right. I had no respect for myself for having had an abortion. I had no respect for myself for having had sex because my father had told me I never should and I didn't listen to him. I was a whore; everybody told me that. So I figured, "I guess that's what I am; this is what I'm supposed to do."

Suicidal thoughts were a regular part of my being during that time. Every night before I went to bed, I would pray that I wouldn't wake up in the morning. I thank God now, every day, that I lived through it. I always have thought that I must have had an angel assigned to me—a case worker.

When I first ran off, my mother had reported me as a runaway. She knew that I was involved in adult films and she told them. All they said was, "We have a case going on this and we will act on it." It took three years to act on it. Three years! My mother went down to that police station three different times and called dozens of times. Every time she called they said, "There's a case going on. That's it. There's nothing we can do right now. We don't have sufficient proof." Once she took a magazine down and slapped it right in their face. They said, "How do we know it's her? It says somebody else's name. We're gathering information." That's what they always told her. But I never knew this at the time. I always thought that she didn't care because she wasn't there. I never saw her, I didn't visit her. I would call her in the middle of the night and hang up, just to hear her voice.

When I was eighteen, the police finally found me. They never arrested me, but they handcuffed me, put me in a car, and took me downtown for questioning. They had my birth certificate and dragged up the whole underage thing. When they took me in, I started crying. I wasn't crying because they were taking me in—I just couldn't believe that somebody was finally doing something.

Then one of the cops said the cruelest thing. He said, "What are you crying for? You're going to be a star. Everyone's going to know your name by tomorrow." I had no idea what he was talking about. It didn't even occur to me that it would be a national scandal. I didn't understand what he was saying. I remember I looked at him and he said, "We're here to help you." And I said, "You're just too fucking late." That's really how I felt. It had been three years. Already a part of me was dead. Looking back on it now, there was so much that was gone by age eighteen, I was a cold, dead woman.

The next few months were really tough for me and my mother, but she showed me the ultimate love once the trials began. Prosecutors all over America were trying to get me to testify. Every time some idiot sold one of my X-rated tapes, I'd get a subpoena. The prosecutors wanted me to appear, not because they needed my testimony, but because I'm press; I'd bring them publicity.

My psychiatrist said I was mentally incompetent to testify. She said I would have a nervous breakdown. Every time I had to so much as talk about my life in adult films, I went crazy. But the prosecutors didn't care. They were totally insensitive. They wanted me to view those awful films. I've never seen one of them. Not ever.

My mother went to court and a judge ruled that if they needed to identify me in those films, my mother could do it; and she did. She appeared in courts in more than ten cities for me. She had to look at those films, but the deal was, she wouldn't have to see anything where I was undressed. All she'd have to see was my face.

While my mother was appearing for me in courts, I started therapy. The first three times I went to the therapist, I cried the entire time. For the first six months, I hated myself completely. I hated the fact that I was going through all of this. I didn't want to be in therapy. I felt like I was forced to be there. Everyone was telling me I had to go. For the first time in my life, I was afraid that I was going to die. I couldn't stand to face all the pain.

Six months after I started, my first breakthrough happened. I finally forgave myself for everything that had happened in my life. The number of men that I had slept with was probably my biggest head trip. I felt like I had screwed half the world. That was a very difficult thing to deal with. It's been really hard for me because even today, I'm constantly being punished because of the way I look, my sexuality. When I was younger, I didn't even know what it was. When I was a teenager, I used it to punish myself because everyone told me that's what I was. Now, as an adult, I'm punished for it because of what I did in the past. So, I've never really been free of that. What happened to me was the most natural thing in the world. It all fits. That's what I was taught. To me, sex was always my punishment, so it was only natural that I punish myself with it. I think that the whole reason I stumbled upon X-rated films and that entire way of life was a direct result of my childhood.

I also began to understand why my father was the way he was. It was his head trip; it wasn't anything I was doing. It was his inability to communicate properly that caused all of these crazy notions on my part. I came to terms with that and I also accepted the fact that when I did X-rated films and I was involved in that world, it really was another person. It was a drugged-up young girl who didn't care, who wanted to die, and that was my form of suicide. To be able to say, "I'm not like that and I wouldn't do that today" really freed me. I know I'm not the kind of girl that would walk into a bar and pick up every guy there. I'm not like that; I have very high morals. I have very high self-esteem today. To be able to let that go really helped me.

Even with all the help I was getting, I still felt so many people were against me. When I was eighteen and nineteen and trying so hard to be an actress, "A Current Affair" and "Hard Copy" would do horrible features on me, how I was such a bad person. It seemed like no one wanted me to succeed, to be worth anything. Everyone said, "Your life is over! You're a porno star; you'll never be anything." I got angry. I said, "This is what people have been telling me all my life. I'm tired of listening to you. I'm going to go to school. I'm going to learn how to act and I'm going to become a huge star just to piss you off."

It took me three years of therapy and all kinds of real soul-searching to stay clean, not to be addicted to drugs—that was a huge problem for me. And then to love myself, to find someone I would let into my shell, and even to fall in love and get married. For me, the last three years of my life have been absolute bliss. My wedding made up for all the bad things that have happened to me.

I had a storybook romantic wedding with the long, Rapunzel-like gown and six bridesmaids; it was my fairy tale come true. He didn't make my whole world better—he came in after that—but he was part of what I wanted.

I met him on the set of *Cry-Baby*. He was the prop master. He's the nephew of the film's director, John Waters. Doing *Cry-Baby* was another form of therapy for me. Everybody on that movie had a history. Patty Hearst played my mother. Iggy Pop, Susan Tyrrell—there were so many people who had had problems. For the first time in my life, no one judged me. All of a sudden I felt like I could do anything. It was so nice to be there and to be a teenager. Aside from the fact that I was getting credibility as an actor, it gave me back my childhood. I was a teenager in the movie and I had books and school clothes and I was back in high school, which was something I never got to finish; I was like a kid. I was in love with this boy. The first time he kissed me, I was scared to death.

Today everything feels wonderful. I've been married a year and a half and it's great. I have this wonderful feeling—sometimes I get in the tub and I giggle like a little girl. I've got my husband and he's the only man who's touched me in the last three years—that's a bizarre feeling. I like the fact that we're faithful to each other.

I think for whatever reason it happened to me, it was supposed to happen. It's definitely given me my quest for my life. As much as I want to be an actress and I want to do things with my career, that's not my quest. The most important thing in my life is changing the status of our kids in the world.

I am very active with Children of the Night, an organization that helps teenage prostitutes and drug addicts. I want to continue to be very active in that and do my part to make a difference in what's happening to our children in this world. I figure that if I can do that, it's worth everything I've gone through. Just being able to talk to these kids and see their faces, to look into their eyes and see them realize that they are not alone, lets me know that I've made a difference in their very scary world.

It's an inspiration to them that I made it out. They look at me differently than they look at their counselor, because I was there. I was one of those little girls out on the street, on the corner. There's a big difference between that and a woman who is caring and loving but who's never been there. They respect that more.

I want to have a child of my own someday. When I do, it's going to be the right time and I'll always be there. I will teach her self-esteem and I will never let her be exposed to things I've been exposed to. I know I would never let anyone do that to my kid. I'll probably have her tied to my back until she's fifteen!

When she's old enough to understand, I'll tell her everything. Because I'm very proud of getting out and living through it. I'm proud of who I am today. I may be only twenty-three, but I think I'm a hell of a woman.

Forgiveness is a gift you give yourself.

Cheryl Crane

AS THE DAUGHTER of movie star Lana Turner and Steve Crane, Cheryl Crane was virtually born in the limelight. But she gained unwelcome notoriety in her own right at age ten, when she was arrested and tried for the murder of her mother's boyfriend, Johnny Stompanato. Cheryl was never convicted of killing Stompanato, but she was inappropriately punished anyway. She was institutionalized, then sent to reform schools. She had a legal curfew set on her and regular check-ins with her probation officer; all this for being judged innocent.

She chronicled this story in her autobiography, Detour. As you will read in this book, her arrest and unhappy past are long behind her. Today, Cheryl Crane is a successful realtor in Beverly Hills. Openly gay, Cheryl has lived with her lover, Josh, for more than twenty years. Cheryl attributes much of her success and recovery to this long-standing relationship and to the fact that she was able to break the silence about the sexual abuse she suffered as a child in her book.

CHERYL CRANE

*I*T may come as a surprise to a lot of people, but looking back on my life, I'd have to say that the part that caused me the most anguish and lingering ill effects was *not* the terrible loneliness because my mother was always gone, and *not* the Stompanato incident. It was the fact that from the time I was ten years old until I was thirteen I was sexually abused by my mother's third husband, Lex Barker.

After the first assault, Lex said to me, "You know what happens to little girls who tell? They get sent away to juvenile hall and never see their parents again." He played into my deepest fear: abandonment. I didn't know what to do. I felt I had no one to turn to. So I remained silent for the next three years and Lex continued to abuse me sexually on a regular basis.

As a child, abandonment was my number-one fear. People who were important to me were continually leaving, usually without offering an explanation. When my mother left to shoot a film, I thought it was my fault she was leaving me. I was nervous around her when she was home. I really believed that if I was very good, she would love me enough to stay. She would be gone for six months at a time, then she'd breeze in for a few days only to disappear again for another six months.

So when Lex threatened to separate me from my mother and grandmother on an even more permanent basis, it played into my deepest fear: being abandoned.

When I was thirteen I finally told my mother about the sexual abuse, and she got very angry. I was so afraid that anger was going to be directed at me. By then I'd come to associate people's disappearing with angry outbursts. It seemed to me that the people I cared about most—my father, my mother—would disappear after terrible arguments. But my mother told me not to worry, that I would never have to see Lex again.

Yet two days later, she took me to the dentist and there he was in the parking lot. I was paralyzed by fright. My mother had told me to put him out of my mind. She'd assured me I'd never have to see him again. Yet there he was. I guess I was still at the age where I assumed my mother was all-powerful. I just couldn't believe that Lex was there again after she'd told me he'd be gone. Seeing him in the parking lot stayed in my mind for a long, long time. I had nightmares about it for years afterward.

I never found out until decades later that my mother had actually confronted Lex about the abuse once I'd told her. At the time, the matter was just never discussed again. That was what made it so difficult on me. Even though Lex was now out of our lives, the situation never felt resolved. It was just one more thing I shouldn't talk about. There was no one to help me sort out my painful feelings.

Those years of abuse were blocked off for me in more ways than I could anticipate at the time. To this day, I can't tell you how I spent my eleventh, twelfth, and thirteenth birthdays. It's as if they never passed. Kids at that age are always pretty focused on birthdays, and to me birthdays were extremely special. My family always made a big deal about them. I looked forward to them more than any other holiday because both my mother and father would be there. But try as I will, I just can't place those missing birthdays. Those three years are total blanks.

When I was in my twenties, I went so far as to have a doctor hypnotize me to see if I could bring those years back. But even he couldn't help me. "Your control is so strong," he said. Control was very important to me for a long time. I thought it was the only way I could protect myself.

I think I would have been a lot better off if I'd been able to talk about these things at the time. But after only that brief discussion I had with my mother when I first told her about Lex, we never talked about it again. It was the same way after the Stompanato incident. I never heard my mother's testimony at the inquest. At the time I wasn't permitted to hear because lawyers didn't want her testimony to influence mine. I wasn't permitted to read the documents. Long after the case was closed I still didn't know that my mother had said, "My daughter was trying to protect me, like any child would do," because she never told me. I never learned any of that until I was writing my autobiography, *Detour*. Then I went back to read the testimony for the first time. What a difference it would have made in my life if I had only known my mother had defended me.

In researching my book, I also learned for the first time that letters of support had been sent to me during the inquest from people all over the country, but I had never been permitted to read any of them. I wasn't even aware of their existence. I had no idea what people thought. I assumed they thought the worst about me because that's how I felt.

When I wrote that book and told my story, I was afraid I would be vilified the way my friend Christina Crawford was when she wrote the truth about her mother, Joan Crawford. I expected to come under that same kind of attack, but that didn't happen. I didn't receive hate mail. To my astonishment, I received mail from people who told me that they related to my story. If only I had understood that growing up. At the time I thought my pain was unique. I'd thought I was the only one. But after writing that book, I realized I was far from being alone.

I always tried not to dwell on the past until I wrote my book. I thought that by not dwelling on those ugly times, I had put them behind me. I failed to realize how much they'd continued to color my life even without me consciously thinking about them. I still had a lot of supressed rage and sadness. Going on tour and having to talk about those incidents was great therapy. For the first time I took a good look at all that had happened to me. It still wasn't pretty, but for the first time I let myself feel the feelings I had avoided for so many years. All my life it had been hard for me to be honest about any of my feelings. I still had bad associations with anger, so I couldn't stand up for myself even when it was appropriate. I had to learn that even if I got mad, no one was going to leave. That was very difficult. It may sound crazy; I was coming to these realizations after twenty years of being in a relationship. I had to learn it was okay to express my feelings. Only then did I begin to feel truly lovable.

When I think of Lex Barker today, I feel nothing. The anger is genuinely gone. There was a time when I pitied him for his illness. He had to be sick to have done what he did to me. I wonder at times if he was abused as a child, and if that is why he molested me. I was just going through the stages of beginning to feel my feelings when I heard that he had died. When I heard the news, I felt nothing. It was like reading about someone I didn't know. There was just nothing there.

It took me a long time to realize that that frightened little girl who'd been afraid to speak out about what Lex was doing still existed inside me. I thought I had dealt with the past. But I had dealt with it as an adult. I didn't know that little girl still existed. When I understood she was still there, I had to go back and mentally put my arms around her and say, "It's not your fault."

Children are so quick to blame themselves. They feel responsible. When bad things happen—be it the divorce of their parents or abuse of any kind—they really need to be told that it isn't their fault.

I have confronted my mother about the big issues that ravaged our family. As an adult, I had to sever the control she had over me. She could really push my buttons; I had to rework my circuitry. Our relationship has changed greatly over the years. We've had many blowups, but they've been healthy ones. I've expressed the anger I bottled up for so long; I don't harbor it or suppress it any more. I've let it go. At first my mother was extremely defensive when I started expressing my feelings, but through talking she's been able to understand that most of that anger isn't directed toward her. Little by little the walls have been torn down.

I don't think my mother has come to terms with her past the way I have, but she's never had the opportunity to understand what it all meant. By writing my story, I knocked down barriers I didn't realize existed. I started to push through the feelings. It was painful to remember, but now that I've come out on the other side of them, I know it was worth the struggle. Now I can stand up for myself and what I really feel without fear. Before, so much of my life had been a facade; I tried so hard to please those around me. I didn't want to push anyone away.

Josh has had a tremendously positive impact on my life. She was the first person to encourage me to get honest. She didn't let me hide behind that artificial facade. She taught me it was okay to get angry. She didn't leave when I got upset. Through her love, I've been able to stop feeling like a soon-to-be-abandoned child for the first time.

Today, I've come full circle. As a child I learned never to trust adults. Now as an adult, the advice I give other people, particularly young people, is to find someone to trust. Most people who are dealing with pain can't do that. But if you can learn to trust, if you can learn to feel your feelings and express them to someone else, you won't find yourself bottled up or being forced into silence the way I was.

Your pain is
the breaking of
the shell that encloses
your understanding.

KAHLIL GIBRAN

Anita B.

ANITA B. IS FORTY-THREE *years old and the admissions coordinator at a women's addiction treatment center. She was horribly abused by her father and has spent most of her life trying to undo the damage. She has courageously shared her story.*

ANITA B.

*W*HEN I was about seven or eight, my mother was in and out of the hospital. One night when she was away, my father said to my older sister and me, "Gee, Mommy's away. Do you girls want to come into bed with me so you won't be scared?" We were both delighted to get into bed with Dad. We snuggled for a while and then he started saying things about what big people do in their bed. "Mommy and I kiss in this bed. Do you want to know the way that Mommy and I kiss? It's real different from the way that we kiss."

We were both starting to feel squirmy. He French-kissed both of us to show us how big people kiss. It was gross. I felt repulsed, but he was my dad and it was supposed to be okay. I was very confused. My sister decided to go back to her own bed. I was pretty starved for affection, so I stayed. He began talking about wet dreams, that men sometimes had wet dreams. I don't remember the rest. I don't know if anything more happened.

I remember nothing else until a year or so later. That doesn't mean nothing happened; I've blocked out a great deal. Dad was a traveling salesman. During summer vacation my mother asked me if I wanted to go to work with my father, drive with him from shoe factory to shoe factory. My mother was just horrendous to be around. She was a rager, and very demeaning. So, getting away from her was exciting.

Being with Dad was great. We had real conversations. He asked me about school and my life and that never happened at home.

Mother always interfered. I was so pleased being with him. We even ate in a restaurant for lunch. We were very poor and so that was a great thrill.

Then the conversation turned to how I felt about boys. He said he wanted to educate me so that boys wouldn't take advantage of me. "It's really important that you learn what happens when you arouse a man because if you do, it's your responsibility to take care of it." He started touching me. He reached inside my underpants and inserted his finger. He wanted me to touch him, and he unzipped his pants to show me what a penis looked like. He kept saying over and over again that I was so special; no one else would understand; no one else could be as grown up as I was. He told me he was touching me so that he could make me feel good. He told me how ecstatic an orgasm was, that he really wanted me to experience it. Then he rubbed me till it hurt, trying to make me have one. I felt like a failure because I didn't.

He had me stroke him while he touched me. He kept a supply of handkerchiefs in the glove compartment, and when he ejaculated, he handed me one to clean myself up.

I was born crippled and wore a brace much of my childhood, so my self-image and my self-esteem were on the floor to start with. I was a bedwetter and my mother humiliated me about it in front of friends. I was also allergic to milk and always had diarrhea or constipation. There was a lot of shame mixed with it. Sometimes I was incontinent. Once, when I was constipated, my mother sat me on the toilet and opened the door, which opened onto the kitchen where the family was sitting. I was to sit there until I had a bowel movement. Hours of total shame and humiliation went by. When I couldn't do it, she was furious and gave me an enema. My sister says she remembers me as a toddler being on my mother's lap and just screaming with frequent enemas.

My father was the best friend I had going. I went to work with him a number of times. And so those times with him were special. I idolized him, romanticized him, and he would say he loved me, and he did it because he loved me. I was so passive and such a people pleaser, I just wanted to do whatever made him happy.

As our car trips continued, he would have me sit next to him so he could have access to me and me to him. I wanted to wear a skirt so that it would make it easier for him. My mother always pushed me to go with him. I think she was afraid that he was having affairs so she sent me with him to prevent that. I felt like I was having an affair with my father and I was the other woman to my mother. There was an excitement in that. And there was a conflict. In essence, it robbed me of having a mother and father.

I don't know how my mother couldn't have known, yet she denies it. She says that she wished she had known; she would have protected me. She said this happened to her when she was a child, too. She was molested by her brothers before she was five and was afraid to tell. But she let those brothers take care of me, and those uncles are the ones I'm having flashbacks about raping me. So, on some level, she had to know. I don't think she wanted me to suffer. I think she had blinders. I think when you're abused and you don't deal with it, don't consciously look at it, you recreate it.

Once a truck drove by, and Dad acted real upset. "Oh, shoot, I bet he saw us. Oh, no, what's going to happen?" I said, "What do you mean? What's the problem?" He said, "Some people won't understand what we're doing. They'll think it's wrong. You don't think it's wrong, do you?" He told me that if people found out they would probably send him to jail; that maybe my mother would kill him or kill all of us, or maybe she would kill herself. I had a very strong message that's still with me: if I tell, somebody dies.

He used language in a slippery way to convince me that it was right. He'd appeal to my intellect and my need to feel special. He used language in a way to make me take responsibility, saying, "You know you don't have to do this if you don't want to. Are you sure you want to do this? I won't do it if you don't want me to." I felt very grown-up at that point in my life, very adult. I figured I knew exactly what I was doing. I was choosing it.

I don't know exactly when it started. I don't know exactly when it stopped. But I know it went on for quite a while, and I know there were times that physically a sexual stimulation was positive. That is something I continue to struggle with today in therapy. I have tremendous guilt about that.

He made a point of saying he would never enter me because he didn't want to get me pregnant; he didn't want to hurt me. I don't remember him doing it, but in regressions with my therapist, it seems like that happened.

Both of my parents studied hypnosis as a hobby, and I was a very good hypnotic subject. Again, that was another way I could feel special. It's entirely possible, and very probable, that there was sexual abuse while I was under hypnosis. That's what has come out through the treatment. It seems that my father's actual programming was, "The more you think about this, the more unclear and faded it will become, the more you will forget it." When I started specifically dealing with these issues a few years ago, that's exactly what happened. We'd get to something in a very deep level and I'd feel emotion, stark terror, tears and everything, and all of a sudden it would just shut down and it would be gone. My therapist is trying to "deprogram" me. It's a struggle, but I'm remembering more and more.

In flashbacks, there are definitely other people involved in sexually abusing me. I had blocked this from my memory, but my sister says that when I was around twelve, there was a man who lived with us for six months. I don't remember him living with us at all. Since I was twelve, I should remember him. I can't dredge up any memory of it.

My sister doesn't have any memories of being molested, but she's just getting into counseling now. We have a lot of similar dynamics. We're both overweight. She doesn't remember much of her childhood at all. In the years she does remember, there are lots of memory gaps.

I left home as soon as I could get out of the house. Except for vacations, I was never home again after I graduated from high school. I didn't date very much, but when I did, I latched onto unhealthy relationships. In college, I went out with professors and older men, married men. They would always put me in a situation where they'd want to make out with me, and I would be outraged and say no. In looking back, I guess I repeatedly found opportunities to say no. Then at age twenty-five, I fell in love with a guy and I made a conscious decision to have intercourse for the first time. I thought of myself as a virgin, but when we finally had sex, I remember thinking, "God, this isn't anything." There was no pain; there was nothing. I didn't think about it, but I probably hadn't been a virgin. That relationship lasted five years and it was very unhealthy. The man I was involved with was an alcoholic.

As soon as I got into the relationship, I immediately plummeted into a tremendous depression. I started seeing a psychiatrist because I couldn't figure out what was wrong with me. I was miserable. I was conflicted about everything. My relationship with my boyfriend kept telling me that I had problems, that I was neurotic, and that I couldn't be sexual. But, for the first six months, I never told my psychiatrist that I had been molested because I didn't think it was important.

That was the first time I told another human being. He put me in group therapy and encouraged me to tell them. Suddenly there was this group of men and women who knew and that is when my healing began. Up until then, I still believed that I had chosen it, and that I had gone along with full knowledge. I distinctly remember going to my father and saying, "You know, Dad, I want you to know that seeing the psychiatrist has nothing to do with you and me." I wanted to protect him. Even now I'm sometimes overwhelmed by this desire to protect him. Denying the abuse allows me to hold on to the illusion that he cared about me. Deep down there's a little girl who still thinks it's her fault. I know it's not. That's the struggle: keeping a clear head about responsibility. In group, I started to recognize that what he had done to me was an injustice. Now I'm finally starting to feel some anger toward my father, but it's still a struggle.

My father has admitted he did it. At first he denied it, and then he admitted it in a very distorted way. He said that it started when I was in high school and it ended when I was in college when he took me to a motel. In fact, he took me to a motel when I was around eight or nine. My mother got angry with me because she thought I should have known better in high school. I had to tell her it wasn't that way. It made me feel so angry.

Later, my father said, "I'll do anything you want me to do." But when I asked him to go to therapy, he refused. A friend of mine, a social worker, offered to see if my father would give any information that would be helpful in my therapy. After meeting with him, she thought he was very slippery and polished and charming. At one point, she actually found herself feeling bad for him. She told him, "It must have been so hard for you reaching out for your daughter, the only one you could love because your wife was so unavailable to you." He said, "Oh, it had nothing to do with love. It was just about lust." When I heard that, I became enraged because he had me convinced it was about love, and that little child still believed that. As long as I believed it was about love, I could somehow rationalize it. When I found out it wasn't, I just felt completely used. When she asked him if he had hypnotized me to have sex, he said, "You can't make someone do something they don't want to do." And I think that's a real sideways way of saying, "Yeah." He got real red and angry and frustrated, and closed down at that moment.

I'm still dealing with all the aftereffects, recognizing how much it has impacted my life. I still have a raft of compulsive behaviors. I overeat, overspend, just overdo. I'm a chronic people pleaser. I have this tremendous need to feel special. I'm terrified of relationships. Any time a man flirts with me, I run the other way. I've never been married. I've wanted to be, but I have made a commitment to myself after that one relationship that I wouldn't get into any more until I got my shit together. I want closeness; I want intimacy; but there's all that ambivalence. God forbid I should arouse someone; then I'd have to take care of him. I haven't had sex since I was thirty . . . about thirteen years.

In so many ways my parents have taken so much from me. I know I'm intelligent and I make my own choices now. But that subconscious core programming is so insidious. That's the struggle I'm in and I'm going to do the necessary work for as long as it takes to achieve healing, balance, wholeness. I no longer want to live my life at a slow idle, feeling shamed, constantly the victim. I've been carrying it all my life and I need to stop carrying it, and live a full life.

I am your child
Wherever you go
You take me too
Whatever I know
I learn from you
Whatever I do
You taught me to do
I am your child
And I am your hope
I am your chance.

"I AM YOUR CHILD"
BARRY MANILOW
and MARTY PANZER

Dan Sexton

DAN SEXTON IS THE director of Child Help, Child Abuse Hotline, and National Survivors of Child Abuse and Addictions Programs. He is a therapist and trains other therapists in the areas of abuse, recovering parents, and recovering alcoholics. He lectures extensively and has just written his first book, The Survivor's Guide: Help for People Recovering from Abusive Addictions.

DAN SEXTON

$\mathcal{I}$ am one of those survivors who had all my memories. I didn't have blank periods where I couldn't remember what happened to me. The first time I talked about the physical and emotional abuse in my family, I was very blasé. I didn't think it was that big a deal. I figured it was stuff that happened to a lot of people, but I definitely knew the sexual abuse was something else. I knew it made me feel real different.

In my family we always trusted and respected grown-ups. We never argued with them, never disagreed; grown-ups were all-powerful. Part of being a good little gentleman was presenting yourself well. We always shook people's hands and looked them directly in the eye, and we didn't argue.

I knew Tom* for three years before the abuse started. He was a family friend and my dad's assistant when he was the athletic director at a university. Tom was like a big brother and often babysat when my parents were out for the evening or gone for the weekend. I looked up to him a lot. He was one of the few men around who wasn't a real "jock-oriented" guy. He gave me a different perspective on men. He always laughed a lot. He played games with me when other kids wouldn't want to. I trusted him very much. I was not a very aggressive kid at that age. I was little at twelve, probably five feet, maybe ninety-five pounds, with these

*Not his real name.

245

ears that stuck out. I was very naive-looking and a pretty passive, quiet kid, particularly around adults.

When I was twelve years old, Tom was in his twenties. One night he let me stay up late with him reading and talking, and he reached over and started to rub my leg. That was okay; but as he moved up into my crotch area, it began to feel real strange. Then he took my hand and put it on his crotch and he had an erection. I remember trying to pull my hand away, but he would not let me pull free. I kept pulling and finally he let go. I got really nervous and sat there for a couple of minutes very confused, not understanding what all this was about. He rubbed my back and did all that kind of stuff, reassuring me that everything was okay. I said, "I've got to go to bed," and went into my bedroom.

I remember trying to calm my heartbeat down enough so I could go to sleep. I buried my head in the pillow and went to sleep on my stomach. I don't know how much longer it was, but I heard the door open. I tried not to pay attention, but then I felt pressure as my head was pushed into the pillow. Tom anally raped me. I remember the excruciating pain of him entering me—it was like the area went numb after my body went into shock, and I just remember focusing so much energy on trying to breathe. I was afraid I was going to suffocate because my head was pushed so hard into the pillow. I kept slowly trying to turn my head so I could get some air. That's all I remember about the incident—just trying to breathe. He went out of the bedroom and I just lay there limp. I had no idea why all that happened. For about a month after, I bled every time I went to the bathroom. It was a constant reminder for me. I didn't tell anyone.

Tom was around the house a lot. I was very uncomfortable. I was very frightened of him, very confused. He always tried to get me off alone, tried to separate me from my ten brothers and sisters as best he could. But I avoided it and pushed him away because I knew he wouldn't push the issue with all the family around. I never had sex with him again in a physical form, but he forced me on a regular basis to call him and entice him to a climax. He'd say, "I want you to call me by Wednesday of this week. If I haven't heard from you, I'm going to do this to one of your brothers or sisters, or I'm going to tell your friends you're doing this with some gay guy, or I'm going to cut the brakes on your parents' car.'' The things that were most painful to me were that he would threaten to rape one of my brothers or sisters and that he might tell other people. I was starting to build a reputation as an athlete and had been written up in the local papers. Tom threatened to go to newspaper guys who were sports figures and tell them that he caught me "blowing" some guy in this area outside our house. I was forced to call him.

I would always wait until the very last day that he said to call. I never called him on Sunday, Monday, or Tuesday. I always waited until Wednesday. I would be so anxious. The tension would build until that date and all through the day while I tried to get up the courage to do it. It was difficult because there were always other people in the house. I would sneak into the back room across the hall from my bedroom, call him, and talk very quietly.

He would say, "You know what to say; just get me excited;" or he'd make me say, "I like your big dick," and how much I liked him having an erection, all those kinds of comments. This went on for four years.

I was doubly uncomfortable because the telephone was across from the bedroom I shared with my older brother Tim, and I didn't know how to hide this from him. I found out years later he heard a lot of the conversations and he just thought I was into some weird stuff as a kid. He had no idea it was all this sexual abuse stuff. He carried this judgment about me for a lot of years. We were able to clear it up and deal with it much later, as we started to deal with our family abuse.

When I was about fourteen and it had been going on for a couple of years, I began to hit puberty, and I remember a few different times talking to him on the phone and finding myself getting somewhat of an erection and being very confused by that. It made me such a mess. I had no idea what that was about. I had no understanding that this was a learned behavior and that I had accommodated to protect myself. I had such incredible guilt about it. But I remember stopping it. I separated from it. I was not going to be present when I was on the phone with him. I learned to disassociate. I had two or three different routines down that I would use with him on the phone that seemed to be his favorites that would entice him faster so the phone call would end. I went for whatever would get him excited the quickest to get off the phone. Generally, it was about him wanting to have anal sex with me. I'd say, "Oh, it's going to feel so good to feel you put that up my butt." That kind of stuff. Or he would talk about the idea of holding me down and putting his erect penis in my mouth and just forcing it in my mouth.

Periodically he would find ways to isolate me in the house or I wouldn't realize he was there, and I would feel him press up against me with an erection. He would keep me pressed there so I couldn't get away from him, and he'd say, "You know how much you like this. Why don't you quit fighting it?" Sometimes he'd show up at sporting events in which I was competing and give me this little sick smile to let me know he was there.

My sense is that he was a mess. I don't think he was gay or not gay; I think he was a guy who preyed on kids. From what I found out years later, he had been sexually abused as a child. He had gone into the seminary and was apparently raped and molested in the seminary as well.

I used to lie in bed at night believing that it was my fault, that somehow if I hadn't been so nice to him or maybe if I'd been nicer, he wouldn't have done this. Or if I'd been more assertive and said no, this wouldn't have continued to mushroom the way it did. I would wonder why there wasn't somebody I could tell about this who would understand. How come he picked me and not one of my brothers or sisters? There were times when I would lie there knowing the night was coming when I had to call him again and I would think, "God, I wish it was Timmy or Michael; I wish it was anybody else." It didn't even matter what they might go through.

I not only had that going on, but I also had an abusive, alcoholic father. My mother drank, too, but my dad was the one who had the drinking problem during those years. My mom came from a very wealthy family. She gave birth to twelve children, eleven of whom lived, and left New York and all of her family support to move to California, a place where she felt very isolated. She was dealing with an alcoholic husband who couldn't seem to hold a job down.

There were times when we lived on welfare. It was a very difficult period and she had no tolerance for stress. The physical and emotional abuse at home was tremendous. Tom knew that I was living in an out-of-control environment and took advantage of that.

I couldn't go to my parents about him. They were not the kind of parents you could sit down and have an intimate conversation with. It was very structured and yet at the same time, it was an incredibly loving family. So it added even more to my confusion. Here were very loving people who at a moment's notice could turn into these violent, angry people. We never knew why or who was going to get it. All hell could break loose. Generally it was because of financial stress and somebody would get it. When we walked through the back door of my house, the first thing we asked of one of the other siblings was, "What kind of moods are Mom and Dad in?" and then we adjusted accordingly.

The physical and emotional abuse going on at home was a nightmare. If I wasn't the one being beaten, I was forced to listen to my brothers and sisters screaming for help. It made me so angry. The number of times I was at home listening to someone in my family be hit or put down, knowing I couldn't do anything about it, filled my body with an incredible rage.

If I acted out on my parents, I would get beaten up badly by my father. If one of my siblings tried to protect another by going after my mom or dad—whoever was doing it—he or she got beaten for interfering. Once, two of my sisters were yelling for Timmy and me to come help them. We got halfway up the stairs and stood there between rage and absolute terror, listening to these people screaming out—and it was bloody screaming.

Another time Timmy called my dad and told him that Mom had lost control and he better get home. My dad got home and Timmy got beat up. So we knew we couldn't go to our parents and we couldn't intervene. We could only listen to it and be thankful it wasn't us and hope it would end quickly.

I used to lie awake and wonder if I was a weird kid. I used to cry and wonder why Tom picked me out. I used to wonder if I was gay; and if I was gay, I must be sick and perverted because that's what I had always learned as a kid. But I could never let anybody know, so I had to be overstated. I was always a real popular kid. I was class president three out of four years in high school. I was a big athlete on the football and wrestling teams. All the girls liked me. I always had the best-looking girlfriends, the cheerleaders. At the same time, I was a guy who ran around and beat people up away from the house. I stole things and did drugs. I lived a dual personality.

As a Catholic, when I went to confession, I never mentioned any of what went on. I disassociated from it, separated from it. I learned as a kid how to convince myself that lies were truth, because I felt so much of my life was a lie. We always had to present this wonderful image to the public wherever we went as a family, yet I knew what was going on at home.

Finally, when I was sixteen, my parents were beginning to see that Tom (my abuser) had a drinking problem. He was not around the house as often any more, so he didn't have access to me as much. He was always around at celebrations and big family functions, but he didn't babysit as often.

He terrorized me from the ages of twelve to sixteen. It never happened to any of the other kids in the family. It stopped for me when I began to see him paying attention to my younger brother. I saw the look on his face and thought, "Oops, Michael is eleven years old now. He's gotten bored with me." I was thrilled that he was bored with me, but I couldn't let him hurt my brother. By the age of sixteen I had grown physically. Plus, I had spent five or six years living in this crazy house where my anger was at an all-time high.

I remember pulling him aside and enticing him into thinking we were going into the back room to have sex. Instead, I pushed him up against the wall and said, "If you ever touch me or anyone in my family, I will kill you. Period." And I meant it. He said, "Bullshit," and grabbed my crotch. I grabbed his hand and twisted his arm so hard I could have sworn I broke it. "You will die." I wasn't loud; I was absolutely dead serious and he knew it. He kind of laughed it off and walked out of the room, and that was it.

I felt such incredible relief, but I was so angry at the same time. To get to a point where I felt like I could kill somebody scared me.

I had that same rage for my parents many times—a feeling like I could have killed them when I watched them do what they did to one of my brothers and sisters. I turned my anger on sports.

In my junior year in high school, I put three different football players out for the season. On that football field I was known as the maniac of the team. I was always the hardest-hitting, most out-of-control guy that they had. The first player I put out was the big star quarterback for another team. He ran a bootleg and I was waiting for him. He was about ten yards up the field and decided to try to run me over. He didn't know what an angry kid I was; and as I hit him, I exploded. I remember hearing a loud pop and I knew it wasn't on my body. I was a little dazed when I got up, but he was lying there groaning. The stretcher came out, took him away, and the whole team, including the coaches, was screaming, patting me and congratulating me. I felt awful that I had done this to somebody, that I had the ability to injure somebody this badly. In fact, I saw this kid at the end of the year during the league track final and he was still on crutches. He hated me and I understood why. But at the same time, everyone around me supported what I had done as a clean, legal hit and that was just the breaks of the game.

In my family some of the worst violence was around the dinner table. The members of my family are the world-champion fast eaters because of it. Our faces were down and we'd just eat. We had to eat everything on our plates because we couldn't get up until we did. That's what we would focus on while someone was being abused. We didn't dare turn around and stare at them being hit. We would hear them cry and hope it would end fast. It was often with fists, but other times with the front and back of the hand. My mom would break skin. Actually, my mom was far more physically abusive to my sisters than my dad ever was to the boys. The girls would bleed or get bruises or cut lips or a broken tooth or a black eye.

I went to college on a football scholarship. I basically put the sexual abuse behind me. I didn't even really think about it much. I was away from home and at that point it was all I wanted. I was a total maniac. I went to classes just enough to stay eligible. Otherwise, I played football, had a lot of sex, and never really got intimate with anybody. I was able to be intimate with friends but never with anyone I was having sex with.

The shit started to hit the fan for me several years later, in my later twenties. I had five or six knee operations over the course of a year and a half, which basically killed the acting and performing career I had pursued.

I went back to school and found that I really liked it. I did an internship at Camarillo State Hospital and found that everyone I was working with had been abused as a kid. I began to think, "Oh, my God, this could have been me."

I began to see some of my behavior getting in the way at that point in terms of relationships with people. I was very defensive. I was a total know-it-all. I always had the right answers. Nobody could outsmart me. If I didn't know the answer, my bullshit was so good I could convince you I knew what I was talking about. I could always back people away. Nobody ever got in touch with what my real pain was. The turning point for me was when I finally got tired of my life not working. I got sick and tired of being sick and tired. I got tired of relationships that didn't work. I got tired of not having what I wanted. I got tired of living this lie with my family that everything was okay when we'd get together and it would feel so awful. I got tired of not being about to cry in front of people because of what it might mean. I got tired of all the judgments I carried around about other people. I got tired of not understanding why I did the things I did and acted the way I was acting. I wanted to change and I wanted to understand what it all meant.

Today, because of the help I was fortunate to get, my life is no longer about holding on to old stuff against people. I spent too much of my life doing that. The more I hang on to old issues and feelings, the more energy and power it takes away from me.

A lot of positive things have come out of this. I have learned that it is very important how we raise our children. When you hit a child, you teach that child to resolve conflicts through hitting. You are training kids to have an inappropriate way of communicating with each other. Hitting never has to happen. As parents we need to spend more time talking to our kids in a loving, supportive, and firm fashion. As a sexually abused child, I lived with shame, guilt, and confusion. It affected every aspect of my being until I got help. But out of this chaos came the opportunity to be a fulfilled person. Today I am right where I want to be, and through my work as a therapist, I am able to pass on the information I have learned from my past abuse. I am able to help those with similar histories to turn it around. People have to know that by facing their pain, they will forever be a part of a voice; and through that voice of recovery, no one will ever have to suffer in silence any more. We all deserve to feel lovable, worthy, and deserving.

Be like the bird,
who halting in his flight
on limb too slight
feels it give away beneath him yet sings,
knowing he has wings.

VICTOR HUGO

Kris Lowden

KRIS LOWDEN IS *thirty-nine years old and only recently remembered the sexual abuse in her childhood. She was a troubled child and no one, including Kris, understood where her seemingly bottomless well of anger was coming from. Her abuser was someone she trusted and depended upon. Later in life, anger and issues of trust and control plagued her, thwarting her every chance at happiness.*

KRIS LOWDEN

I didn't realize that I had been sexually abused until I was twenty-eight, about eleven years ago. I was talking with my husband, my brother, and his wife about my grandfather and family, and I just blurted out, "By the way, Grandpa molested me." That's how it came out. I hadn't even been consciously aware of it before I said that.

My grandparents had quite a large home. When we visited, all the adults gathered in the kitchen, drinking, playing cards, having fun. Everybody was doing something. My three brothers, everybody was involved with somebody else, and I was in the living room with Grandpa. That made me feel special.

My grandfather and my father were alcoholics. My father was just building up in his alcoholism. The disease is progressive. My mother wasn't drinking, but she was right there as an enabler; so was my grandmother to my grandfather. They would put the whiskey on the table and go from there. I think my grandfather probably knew if he could distract my father with booze, he could get to me. Alcoholics are so clever and they think it all the way through. It's all about how to get what they want.

It started when I was six or seven. From the kitchen at my grandparents', you couldn't see from one room to the other. My grandfather used to lie on a couch in the alcove and watch TV. He asked me to come and lie down with him. He'd put his arm around me in an affectionate way, but it held me down. Then he put his

259

hands in my panties and felt my genital area. I also believe that he put my hand in his pants. It went on for three or four years.

When I was in the bathroom, my grandfather would come in and pretend he needed something from the medicine chest. And he would look at me. So there was an element of fear. I wasn't quite sure of how far he would go or what he wanted. I felt guilty, I felt I should have been able to stop it from occurring again.

As an unconscious payback, I would steal his favorite pens from his desk—his sacred area. I knew this was special to him and I wanted to intrude on a private area. Of course, at nine, I didn't understand that, but I realize now that's how I acted out some of my anger.

I felt a lot of respect for him, but I clearly remember him as a crabby man. He was the master of the house. He always got his way. He had wild mood swings. He'd go from playing and singing with us kids to barking and bellowing, and we'd just want to cower. He also had a reputation as a ladies' man. My mother's mother was a widow and she refused to stay in the kitchen with my grandfather because he would feel her, touch her breasts. Everybody knew about it, but they treated it like a joke. It wasn't taken seriously. I think this is why I never told anyone about it. I was probably afraid they wouldn't believe me.

I felt very different from other children. I felt unloved by my father. He ridiculed and criticized me for years. One night when he was very drunk, he said, "Kristine, you are my only daughter; you need to be perfect." And of course, I couldn't be, so I was always under a lot of criticism.

I went through many years of acting out. Thank God I'm alive today. I graduated from high school in 1970. It was the drug culture. I was a hippie. I did probably every drug that anybody could make—marijuana, cocaine, LSD. The first drug that I did was alcohol. Alcohol numbed me. My father is an alcoholic, and my grandfather, too. But that wasn't the road I was going to take. I stopped that.

I've been fortunate enough to have been gifted with a really nice husband and partner. I met him when I was twenty-one, and we married when I was twenty-eight. I've been open with him. In fact,

I think his presence allowed me to regain those memories. When he touched me in the same way my grandfather had, it triggered negative feelings that I didn't understand. So I started talking to him about it and he was really there for me.

I wondered where my parents were when it was going on. That they were so physically close and couldn't stop it made me very angry. It wasn't until I understood the progressive nature of the disease, and how families react to it, that I knew my mom and dad were just as sick as my grandfather.

I finally reached a point where I could discuss this with my mother. My dad is a maintenance drinker, and I have chosen not to talk to him unless he's completely alcohol-free. When I told my mother, she wasn't surprised, but she was angry that it had happened. But more than that, she was really glad that I had gone to treatment and that I could talk to her about it. Then the most amazing thing happened. She told me she had been molested by a neighbor when she was little. We talked for a long time about what it was like, how she felt, what it was like for me. Since then, she has told my father what I had shared with her, and that's okay with me. Last week she went home and told two of my brothers about the molestation in her childhood. She said, "There wasn't a day that went by that I did not think of this man. Now I have days that go by that I don't think of him."

When I think back on the little girl, little Kris, I feel a lot of love. I took her out of this. She's not there anymore. She's no longer on the couch. She's in my heart, and we spend time together. She's no longer in the places that were painful and hurt her. I know I still have a lot of growing to do, but it's not scary to me anymore.

It has truly been worth the pain. There are safe people and doctors. There is light at the end of the tunnel.

I think it's very important that people question their therapists, question treatment centers, and say, "What is your experience with this? What are your qualifications?" Slow down and remind yourself that you're living today, and help is available.

Forgetfulness is a form
of freedom. Remembrance
is a form of meeting.

KAHLIL GIBRAN

Richard Berendzen

ACCORDING TO HIS COLLEAGUES, *Richard Berendzen was the best president that American University ever had. He was the man to whom others came for counsel, who, for all outward appearances, was totally in control: a distinguished scientist, educator, and community leader. No one, not even those closest to him, suspected for a moment the terrible secret of his distant past that he concealed. Nor could they have guessed his more recent secret—one that would change the entire way the community regarded him.*

In May of 1990, Richard Berendzen pleaded guilty to making indecent phone calls. He had answered an ad in the Washington Post *advertising for child care in a private home. The woman who answered had a tap put on her line which eventually traced the calls to Dr. Berendzen's office at the university. Over a two-week period, authorities tapped and recorded thirty to forty calls.*

Why would a respected and accomplished man endanger all he had worked for to harass a woman he had never met with graphic descriptions of sexual abuse of children? What no one knew then was that Berendzen's bizarre calls were symptoms of a post-traumatic disorder provoked by the sexual abuse he endured earlier in his life. These phone calls revealed a sort of horrible fascination about what had happened to him as a child and whether those things were happening to others.

When asked about the specifics of the phone calls, Richard would only say they were "quite inappropriate and grotesque." The person on

265

the other end of the phone became a surrogate for his own victim-izer—a person he both trusted and loved, hated and despised.

Up until the time of this scandalous and very public debacle, Dr. Berendzen had led a life of service and commitment to other people. He had evinced nothing but high moral standards and the utmost trustworthiness throughout his distinguished academic career. Because of the respect he had garnered, the shock to the community was tenfold.

But the shock to Richard Berendzen was life-shattering. All that he had worked for during his lifetime was unraveling. He was terminated by American University as president, and ridiculed in the press and media by those passing judgment with no knowledge or understanding of the effects of abuse and its manifestations later in life.

Even though Dr. Berendzen's childhood abuse was now creating catastrophe in his life, he still felt reluctant to identify his abuser. This is classic behavior and present in many of the sexually abused adults I have interviewed for this project.

"Often a victim will never identify who his abuser is, because deep down in his mind he believes it is his fault," says Dr. Rader. Abused children feel they are to blame because even though they knew it was wrong, on some level it might have felt good.

Dr. Berendzen has been on a long and difficult journey of understanding and recovery through the help of the doctors at the Johns Hopkins Hospital, noted for its pioneer work in treating sexual abusers and the sexually abused. And through the love and support of his family, he has come to understand his behavior was a result of childhood pain that had never been resolved. With that understanding comes the peace that had eluded him for so many years.

RICHARD BERENDZEN

*A*T age eight, I was sexually abused for the first time. I was introduced to things by both a man and a woman, who brought me into their activity. This activity was not extensive. But I must say, to a child it was profoundly confusing. I wondered what was going on and why I was a part of it. "What in the world is this all about," I'd ask myself. Abruptly, it ended, with no explanation, no nothing.

I probably thought I had no choice. When you're a child, adults are very ponderous and controlling. Nobody swore me to secrecy; no discussion, no remarks. Nothing. Therein lay part of the bafflement. Three years later, at age eleven, a woman very close to me introduced me to adult sex, and it happened a number of times. The most baffling aspect of it at the time was, "Why? Why is this happening? Why me? Why is it happening at all? Why? Why? Why?"

Let me put this in proper context. There was not one word ever spoken except, "Come here." No, "I'm doing this because," no, "I want to show you something," no, "You must never tell anyone," no, "This is our special, hidden secret just between us," no anything. Then afterward, silence. In the interlude between one occasion and the next, I would wonder, "Will there be a next? Do I want there to be a next?" I dreaded it and somewhat ashamedly, I also wanted it. And that's part of my pain.

There's was a terrible confusion. You see, at age eleven, I had not yet reached puberty, but I was getting close. So for me, girls were "yucky." Two years later they weren't, but at that stage I wanted to play baseball and football and ride my bike. I didn't even really look at girls. On the other hand, when I was introduced to such mature activities as outright sex, it was stimulating and exciting and repulsive all at the same time. I can remember some of those feelings as vividly as if it were yesterday. It was a simultaneous feeling of shame and embarrassment, of pain and fear, mixed with excitement and pleasure. But mostly it was confusion.

The question of shame agonized me for several years. I kept coming up with a dual response to it. One side of me was embarrassed and never wanted anyone ever to know; not my best friend, not my doctor, not my wife (if I someday got married). Nobody. On the other hand, I felt that maybe I was a step ahead of my peers because a year or two later the boys began to fantasize and talk about girls. They would brag beyond anything that was actually happening. And I would quietly think to myself, "Yeah, well, what do you guys know?"

My ultimate solution was utter denial. I told myself it hadn't happened. I did my best to forget. I refused to think about it and if it ever crept back into my memory, I would think, "Nope, I'm not going to think about that today."

Somewhere around age fourteen or fifteen I began to blame myself: "Maybe I brought this on. Maybe I was the seducer. For heaven's sake, I am a boy. I could have stopped it. Did I ever once say, 'Stop, I don't want this'?" The answer was no. "Did I fight back the way women fight back if they're going to be raped?" No, not at all. I blamed myself for some time.

When the encounter stopped without a word of explanation, I was as baffled as I was when it began. On one hand, I rejoiced that it stopped; on the other hand, I nursed fear it would reoccur.

I married quite young and was a father at eighteen. We were divorced after three years. We both were too young. But I felt a real responsibility to my young daughter. I was determined to try to provide well for her and be a good dad. And the only way I could do that was to study hard and get a decent job. So I worked my way through as an undergrad, majoring in physics at MIT. For my master's and Ph.D., I stayed in Cambridge and went to Harvard.

During all of this I still had a feeling of catching up from childhood and that seemed to push me to work ever harder. There was this defense mechanism I had that made me feel that if I kept not just busy, not just extremely busy, but ultra-extremely busy, I wouldn't have to think about anything that was unpleasant. For a long time, I kept the memory and the confusion pushed out of my mind.

But then a few years ago, I went back home for my father's funeral. When I walked into the room where the abuse occurred, the very room where my father had his heart attack, I felt like I'd been hit by a two-by-four. I walked in there on the most innocuous of missions; I had been asked by the funeral director to pick the suit in which my father would be buried. I looked at the very place where my father died, where I had been victimized, and I took a deep breath. I felt faint, I felt nauseous. I went around the corner to the bathroom, splashed cold water on my face, and put my head between my knees. I breathed deeply for a while to regain my composure. All this took but a few minutes. Once I caught my breath, I went back into the room to complete my errand. All of my old confusion and doubt came back like an avalanche. And sadness, too.

I don't recall exactly the first time I made an indecent phone call—the police and the doctors called them "indecent", not "obscene"—but I think what prompted me to do it was an article about the McMartin alleged child-abuse case in California. I don't know my exact chain of reasoning; I have no idea. But for some reason, I made the first call. I made very few calls at first.

Then in January, 1990, my wife decided I needed to exercise more. She bought me a treadmill, but before I started to use it I went in for a stress test. In the middle of the test the cardiologist asked his assistants to leave the room. He took me into a private office and said, "There seems to be an abnormality in your tracing. I don't know what it means. It could be a fluke. On the other hand, you may have a serious heart problem." After that, my own mortality, no doubt colored by my father's recent death, became my central line of thought. That's when the calls became more frequent.

I answered an ad for child care in a private home. Over a two-week period I made a number of calls. The subject matter of the calls focused on child sexual abuse. The calls were eventually traced to my office. In April of 1990 I admitted myself into Johns Hopkins Hospital. Shortly afterward, I pleaded guilty to two misdemeanor counts of placing indecent phone calls.

I didn't understand what was happening to me. Ninety-nine-point-nine percent of me was the person the world knew. But there was a minuscule portion of me, an odd tic, I just couldn't understand. I told them I would cooperate fully, anything, if they would just help.

Of course, I couldn't have dreamed what was about to happen. They wanted to know about how I'd been treated as a child. It took a lot of time to get to the bottom. They used hypnosis and truth serum and finally the abuse of my childhood emerged. I still couldn't see any linkage. It took many days of intense discussions before I could accept it. I kept asking them how something from so long ago could still trouble me today.

I simply didn't realize what a hostage I was to my own past. There's a paradox in this. My own field was astrophysics. So here I was, understanding a distant quasar, but not the boy still within the man. I didn't realize that as a child grows into an adult, the pain and confusion can linger on. Just because you grow up doesn't mean they go away. I didn't seek help because the confusion didn't seem to bother me anymore. I thought, "Why do it?" Also, I was simply too arrogant. I was too impressed by my own accomplishments. "Hey, maybe somebody else can't solve his problems, but I sure can solve mine."

Gradually I came to understand the chain of events that prompted me to make those calls. The doctors reminded me of post-traumatic stress disorder, a term most associate with returning Vietnam War veterans. When they see a car crash, sometimes they remember napalm in Cambodia. I never dreamed such a thing could be related to me; but when I walked into that room, it was as if a board cracked me across the skull and flattened me against the wall. Going into that room to get a suit for my father is what triggered that kind of reaction in me.

When I was at Johns Hopkins Hospital, they kept asking me about anger. For some reason I didn't get angry very easily. I may get annoyed. I may get peeved. But I don't seem to have deep anger, which large numbers of people have. Perhaps I should. I don't know. But they kept asking me, didn't I have anger towards this woman? I had to say, "No, I don't." This is where it becomes very difficult for me to explain.

I make no excuses for what I did. The child abuse in my life in no way absolves me of those calls. I take full responsibility for what I did. Making those calls was profoundly wrong. Now I know I should have gotten psychiatric assistance. If I had understood then how the abuse I suffered was linked to those calls, I might have sought help. But I didn't, and for that I shall forever be sorry. In an intellectual sense I can forgive myself, but I can't forgive myself in a human sense. I'm a mature professional who should have been able to appreciate the gravity of the situation.

While in the hospital, I discussed with the doctors whether the effects of abuse were different for men and women. My sympathy and empathy for women who are abused are absolute and total, because they are usually abused by a male who is stronger and older and bigger and in control. It must be terrifying and awful for the female. Also, though, I gather that sometimes a young girl may be able to intellectually disassociate from the event. She will pretend that she is in a playground or watching a movie; then later, when the man has left, she can come back into her real mental state again. In the case of the boy participating, just by virtue of the boy's anatomy, he is quite aware of what's happening. It's intellectually difficult for him to say to himself, "I wasn't there," when he knows full well he was.

In both cases it's a painful situation. I give great credit to the women's movement in the last twenty years because women have made it socially acceptable for girls to speak out on these matters. Males, in my view, are behind females in these things. In the 1990s, it's far less well known for males in our society to talk about having been abused. Yet, from the data I've heard, nearly one in three of the women in this country were sexually abused as children and at least one in six of the males were. If those numbers are even close to accurate, then millions of males are doing what I did: pretending, denying, hiding, keeping it a secret.

For a long time, the doctors at Johns Hopkins urged me to explain everything to my wife. I just couldn't. But then finally, one day, I had her come into my room at the hospital. We closed the doors and talked for hours. It was the most painful, emotional conversation of my life. She listened; I talked. I wept; she listened. I talked; I wept. Finally I stopped. When I was finished, there was silence for a moment. Then she cleared her voice and said, "I have three things to say. First, I love you more than ever before. Second, I am angry. I feel intense rage at the woman who did this. And third, you were a victim once. Now you are a victim again because of the first time." My eyes filled with tears. We hugged, feeling closer than ever. And at last I knew a great release and peace.

When I was a youngster, I yearned for my victimizer to apologize to me. When I was fourteen or fifteen years of age, I hoped very much for a frank, honest, and full discussion that would explain to me why it started and why it ended. But that never happened. Now it doesn't need to happen. I now understand the situation well. I also know there are certain things in life you will never know with total clarity. Sometimes you don't need to. If, with professional help, you have explored the matter thoroughly and you finally have resolved the issues for yourself, then you can put it all in perspective. That's probably sufficient.

Today I understand what happened to me as a child. I've talked it through; it's resolved. I don't have lingering questions or doubts. But now I have to deal with all that's resulted from all this—the publicity about me and what it's meant to my life, my position, the blow to my reputation, and what it's done to my family. But I'm reassured, because others have faced far greater challenges, and yet they've come through. So, I'm confident I will, too.

I hope in due course people will know that I am the same person I was all along, the same guy who used to give talks and write papers and chair meetings and work with different groups. The difference now, I believe, is that I understand the linkage of my past with my present. I'm a happier person than before. I feel as if a huge boulder has been lifted from my shoulders. I see things with more clarity and more feeling than I did before. So despite the pain and trauma, maybe in a way, ironically, my life is better now than before. I sure hope so.

The elder of my two daughters taught me something when she said to me one day, "You know, if your body were hurting, people would send flowers; but because your mind is hurting, some people will throw bricks." It was a very special moment for me. I was on a pay telephone in the hospital worried about how she was feeling about all this. It buoyed my spirits and tersely summed up a great deal.

As I look to the future, I'd like to get on with my life. I hope to leave behind the pain, the hurt, the confusion, and the shame. And I hope, in some modest way, that my story will benefit others. I have hope. I have faith. And I believe.

THE GIRL

The girl has no life, no self-esteem
A lonely feeling of a shadow is her
        only friend she can trust.
She can only be herself
But to find out who she is, the
        girl digs deep through memories
        of her distant disastrous
        childhood.
She feels abused, like a piece of
        glass
Crumbled in a hand, each finger sliced
The drops of blood are symbol of her
        unhappiness
Not easy to understand but so easy
        to visualize.
Her sadness grows deeper to the extent
        of feeling like an abandoned dog
Digging through a garbage can and crying
Disappointed in herself, tired, wanting
        just to die.

And the resentment grows, do you understand
        this?

KARIN, 13
Martinez, California, from *Sounds from the Streets:*
A Collection of Poems, Stories, and Art Work by Young People
© National Network of Runaway and Youth Services

Marie Williams*

MARIE WILLIAMS'S TRAGIC STORY *of sexual abuse has robbed her of the basic human right of happiness for the past thirty years. The hurt and confusion are just now beginning to make sense. She always blamed herself, but now realizes that a four-year-old child cannot do wrong. She was forced to participate sexually and then condemned for doing so. Today, through therapy, she is finally understanding and turning her life around.*

*Not her real name.

MARIE WILLIAMS

*W*HEN I was almost four, my father told me to watch him and my mother having sex through his bedroom door. My mother didn't know. I was really in the middle of a terrible triangle. I knew it was wrong and didn't want to hurt my mother. But I was afraid of my father. I didn't really want to please him, I just didn't want to disobey him because I'd get spanked with a leather strap. My dad was a dictator, the ultimate disciplinarian: creative capital punishment. He got my brother and sister to do it, too. Funny, I don't remember talking to them about it at all. You never talk about *it*.

The first guilt I felt was when my mother saw me watching. When she looked at me like that, I knew it was wrong. But she thought it was my idea. That is a cord that has run through my life: she thought it was my idea. That was the beginning of the separation between my mother and me.

At four, I remember him sneaking into my room and doing something to my sister. I also remember him coming to my bed and feeling my body at that same age. He started when we were babies, before we even knew. So it always seemed natural. It wasn't a shock, like one day we just got molested.

Initially, he had me watch him with my older sister. My most vivid memory is of my sister on top of him with me between his legs forced to watch his penis going in and out of her vagina. It was disgusting. This thick, sticky white stuff and this thing going in and out. It was repulsive. I could never watch that again, even today.

I don't remember ever talking about it, even after it was over. At the time I seemed to think she was enjoying it, but now I know she wasn't.

I don't remember the first time he put his penis in my vagina. It just progressed. Having sex goes so much farther than just having intercourse. I was about eight when he was having anal sex with me. That was very painful. I was already having to perform oral sex on him by that age.

That same year, he told me he was going to buy me a pony, which was my dream come true. While he was driving, he suddenly pressed me up against the door so I couldn't get away. Then he put his finger in my vagina and broke my hymen. It was extremely painful. I was screaming and crying. I felt totally exposed, totally vulnerable. I thought everybody from the other cars was going to see. I bled on my underwear. I think my father threw them away. I was totally afraid of my dad.

Dad involved my brothers and stepbrothers in strip games he made us play. We'd throw pennies up against the wall and whoever's penny was the farthest from the wall had to strip. Or card games where you'd have to strip. We all hated it. I don't know how he got us all to do it. He was oppressive, domineering. We were afraid of him, with legitimate reason. Once he threatened me with a loaded gun. We were petrified of my dad, my mother included.

One time he wanted my mother, my sister, and me to go bed together sexually. My mother was so intimidated, totally petrified of my dad. He got me on top of him and my mother was pushing me up and down on him, actually forcing his penis into me while she was crying the whole time. I knew she didn't want to do it, but I thought she was hating me. This wasn't the first time he'd entered me, but I think my mother thought it was. Maybe she realized it wasn't because I would have been screaming. It was so awful. From then on, my mother really abandoned me.

He never drank. Never smoked. His father was a severe alcoholic who physically beat *him*, my grandmother, everybody. And though he never admitted it, he had to have been sexually abused, too. My dad came from a totally dysfunctional family. He confided all this to me, everything except what he did with my sister.

His words were that I was his favorite, I was special. He always picked me to go with him, but being "Daddy's favorite" was so horrible. I was molested every day. When I was ten, before my parents' divorce, he made me promise we would always be together, that we would be secretly married. I knew he was sick and that I'd never get away from him.

I had nobody I could trust. I couldn't go outside of the family. I knew my dad would kill me. Right before my parents divorced, my mother tried to get him to stop. She had tried to help us before, telling us how to say no to him without making it seem like she told us. When he found out, he went after her. After that, she hated me, like I had betrayed her. She even hit me on the head one night when she caught me and him together. Today, we're still not all healed.

When they divorced, we had a choice of whom to go with. My father went into a rage when my sister went with Mom. So, even though two of my brothers and I wanted to go with Mom, we stayed with Dad.

Without Mom, I now had to sleep with my dad. Then he remarried. He was in his thirties. His new wife was about nineteen, from Finland, and didn't speak much English. She didn't know anything at first, but after a while Dad suggested I sleep with them. Eventually we had sex. At first she didn't know, but later, she realized we were having intercourse.

I had an orgasm by my dad, and that was the hardest thing for me to talk about for the longest time. The orgasm itself felt good, but even while it was happening I hated it.

I was fourteen when my dad got me pregnant. I didn't hide it, but I didn't tell anybody either. Nobody at school said anything. I don't remember being pregnant. I just remember the abortion. He didn't want me to go to a hospital. I was four or five months pregnant when he took me to Tijuana. He took me to a woman. She did something, I don't know what, inside of me. I came home, and aborted at home that night on the toilet. I called my stepmother because it was hurting so much. The baby came out in the toilet water. When I think about it, it is so sick. A human life went down the toilet. I wish I could have thrown it at him. She saw it. I don't even know if it was a boy or girl.

My stepmother was both compassionate and angry. I know she and my dad had many arguments. She ended up fighting with me later, because he kept having sex with me. It was easier to blame me than to keep fighting him. She ended up hating me.

After the abortion, my stepmother went to the police and told them he was having sex with me. They came and talked to me at school. I told them they were crazy. I was a great actress. My father had warned me that if I told, our family would be split up, we'd go to foster homes, he'd go to jail, and he'd come looking for me when he got out. I wanted to run away but I was too afraid. The first place he'd look was my mother's. I couldn't go there and was afraid to go out on my own.

I felt very misunderstood. I never hated myself. When I had that abortion, I felt like my body was not mine. I didn't feel responsible. I felt betrayed. Everybody who knew did nothing about it. Even my brothers and sisters said I liked being his favorite. I'm sure they knew we were having regular sex, at least later they did.

As I got older I was getting more and more depressed. My dad saw that. He knew he couldn't keep doing this. I didn't tell him, but I felt suicidal. I never tried to commit suicide. I just wanted to. I tried to figure a way that people would notice so they'd help me, so I wouldn't die. It was a cry for help. I've often felt I wanted to die since then.

He started to leave me alone when I was about seventeen and he started having sex parties in the Valley. He was written up in *Playboy* magazine for having wife-swapping parties. I was embarrassed about the article.

I wanted so much to be loved. I moved in with a girlfriend. I was afraid to be alone. I got on the pill and started having intercourse with my boyfriend after I graduated from high school when I was sixteen and a half. I loved him. He had been really good to me, never forced anything. I wanted to make him feel good like I'd been taught. I'd really been taught how to make a man feel good. I used to go over to his house and have sex on my way to work; that way I didn't have to be alone from the time my roommate went to work to the time I got to my job. Eventually we broke up, because he thought we were too young to go out only with each other. I felt scared. I just couldn't be out of a relationship.

I soon found one relationship after another to be in, but I never found real love. I finally got away from my dad and moved out just before I turned eighteen. At this point, I had very low self-esteem and was pretty disillusioned about the world of men. I thought once I got away from my dad everything was going to be great. At nineteen, I got engaged and, for the first time, I told someone outside the family about the incest. He didn't mind. After that, I started opening up to girlfriends and therapists.

After I was married, I had trouble having an orgasm for a long time. Sex wasn't normal. I would end up feeling like I was with my father. I felt repulsion, yet this was my husband whom I loved. I'd try to remember that at the same time. Finally, I did have an orgasm and felt I was on my way to healing.

I had gotten some answers in therapy. I had been in touch with my father. He told me how he'd changed. He'd gotten religious. But my younger brother told me my dad was trying to get him involved with my half-brother and sister. I couldn't believe it. My therapist warned me that if I told her she'd have to report it. I told her everything.

She reported it. The kids verified it. I called my family, told them Dad was still doing it, that I needed their support and information. They were all still afraid of him but they gave me support. Even my mother. We were all still scared. Three of the kids and my mother gave statements. One brother didn't.

The kids got taken away for a while. My dad didn't go to jail, but got a felony conviction. The whole family and community knew about it. My aunt, who I dearly loved, disowned me when she found out I had started it. I think she believed it and knew it was true, but felt I had ruined our family name. She betrayed me. I was totally crushed.

Always being the victim, always getting blamed has made me try to explain myself all the time, in everything. I don't want to be thought of as a bad person in anything at all. I want to be liked, I want to be loved. I do my best. I work hard. But in the last year I've felt worse than I've ever felt as an adult because I've realized how sick I am, and how far I'd go to protect myself from being alone. I've been married three times. I'm separated from my third husband. I'll get a divorce.

My daughter could fill the void if I gave her a chance, but I don't want to depend on her for that. If she wants to leave, I don't want to hold on to her. We have a very good relationship. I've told her about some of the things that happened to me because I want to protect her. Also, I need her to understand why I've had some problems, and why I'm the way I am.

Several years ago, Dad moved to San Diego to be closer to my two brothers, their wives and kids. He convinced them that he'd changed and they let him live with them. He went to church with them. But while my brothers were at sea with the Navy, my dad abused and sexually molested their kids.

I jumped into it ready for battle. I told their mothers that I'd support them, help them, and go to the police on their behalf if they felt they couldn't. I told them I wouldn't back down. For the first time in my life, I stood face to face with my father and accused him publicly of sexually abusing children. I was thirty-nine. Dad was charged with eighteen felony counts. He got eight years.

I had nightmares about my dad for years. After I started therapy I started talking back to him in my dreams. Then I had him arrested in real life. I don't hate him. I hate what he did with a passion and I could no longer hide my head in the sand and let it continue. I feel sorry for him. I wish he would have been strong enough or smart enough to get help. I will never see him again, but even though he's in jail, I'm still afraid of him.

I love my mother. I wish she loved me more. I think she's trying, but she's limited. She doesn't reach out to me until I reach out to her. She understands the depth of the pain, but just can't handle it. Maybe seeing me reminds her of her failure to protect me.

I'm still trying to get to the bottom of this fear of being alone. Why can't I let it go now? My dad's in jail. I *can* make it through the night without talking to my boyfriend, but I *can't* stay out of a relationship for more than a month. It's hard for me to believe anything can last, or there is anyone I can trust.

My therapist says I am addicted to sex. I probably am. I enjoy it when I'm doing it with somebody I love who I know loves me. Other times I do it for the physical feeling of closeness or the emotional feeling of having two arms to hold me. I'm in touch with my feelings and pain. I don't shut it out. But it is about feeling alive and connected with somebody, anybody. I want someone to help me, anybody but my father. When my girlfriends give me a hug, I'm fulfilled. Sex is supposed to represent love and I'm believing that, over and over again.

I do have hope, but I don't think it's ever going to be okay. Something always sets me off. There's so much sex in this world that I think is inappropriate, so much advertising. I know I've grown and come a long way, but it scares me that I have such a long way to go.

The mind is its own place, and in itself
Can make a Heav'n of Hell, a Hell of Heav'n.

JOHN MILTON
Paradise Lost

Debby Goodman

THE STORY OF *Debby Goodman's childhood is horrible and shocking. How any human being could survive these circumstances is beyond belief. Debby is not only a victim of constant sexual assaults and rapes at the hand of her father, she is also a survivor of a devil-worshipping cult that almost took her life.*

As difficult as it may be to read the following story, it is important to note that this situation is being repeated nightly all over this country with innocent children being stripped of all trust, dignity, and happiness.

Today, Debby is surviving and works as a therapist helping others who have had similar experiences.

DEBBY GOODMAN

*M*Y father belonged to a cult that worshiped the devil. I think that there is a very real possibility that he, too, was abused in a cult as a child. My grandfather was a violent drunk who beat up his wife and children, my father in particular.

My father was a very weak man and very, very screwed up. He had a tremendous amount of unexpressed rage with no idea how to contain or relieve it. I think his participation in the cult was partly his acting out the abuse that had been perpetrated on him and partly a way for him to believe he belonged somewhere, that he was a part of something. It was certainly a way for him to release his rage and feel moments of power. He was in control.

The abuse I suffered at home coincided with my father's involvement in the cult. I was four years old the first time I remember my father coming into bed and molesting me, sticking his fingers in my vagina, my rectum. The rape didn't start until I was seven.

Some children freeze when something is frightening. That's exactly what I did. I would lie there and pretend it wasn't happening. I also got very good at putting my mind someplace else; becoming a part of the wall.

He told me not to tell, to shut up and be quiet. "I'll kill you. I'll kill your sister. I'll kill your mother." It was absolutely terrifying. The movement and the sounds were terrifying, and at that age, I thought he went to the bathroom on me when he had an orgasm. This went on from the time I was four until I was thirteen or fourteen.

I don't know how much you know about cults and cult abuse. Some of this may be really disturbing and hard to hear, but I believe that we have to know to stop this from happening. That is the reason that I'm doing this. These cults are very, very organized, very sophisticated. Powerful people are involved. They have doctors and medical researchers who are highly skilled at brainwashing techniques. They use drugs, hypnosis, terror, and physical pain so that people don't remember, don't tell. They put people into trance states to make them do things or forget things. One of their favorite torture techniques is electric shock. I clearly remember them using it on my mother.

My mother was not a member of the cult and they had to get control over her. I believe that is the reason my sister and I were not killed during any of these rituals; it would have raised some serious questions. They had brainwashed and programmed my mother so that all my father had to do was say some key words and she would go into a trance. Then he would drug her and take us out of the house. I remember whimpering and saying, "Where's Mommy? Where's Mommy?" And my father saying, "Your mother is asleep and she's not going to wake up."

She was also tortured. I remember watching them torture my mother in an electric chair. They were saying to me, "This is what will happen to your mother if you tell what they are doing to you and your sister." Then they'd turn the electricity on. My mother was unconscious through a lot of it and she vomited on herself. They would continue to say things to me like, "You know you want to tell." And I would say, "No, no, I don't want to tell." But of course, I did want to tell. They would say, "You're lying," and turn the electricity up. They are very smart at what they're doing.

They use a lot of drugs in these cults, all kinds of designer drugs—drugs that would alter my consciousness, that would make me paralyzed; that was the worst. I would have terrible nightmares about becoming paralyzed—where I couldn't make my body move but I was fully conscious. It was another severe instance of having no power. My whole childhood was so powerless.

There are different kinds of rituals throughout the year. There's a lot of activity around Christmas and Easter. Ceremonies involve chanting, robes, candles, pentagrams drawn on the ground if it's outside or on the floor if it's inside. There are lots of rituals using blood, human blood.

The devil-worshiping cults believe that children are closest to God and most loved by God, so that to desecrate children is the biggest slap in the face that you can give to God. They kill children, babies. Sometimes they would cut their heads off. Sometimes they would put daggers through their chests, cut their abdomens open and remove their hearts. They did that a lot. They have women in these cults who are breeders—who have children for the purpose of sacrifice. They are delivered by doctors in the cults so there are no birth certificates.

The ways in which the cult terrifies children are unbelievable. I was put in a harness and lowered into a pit full of spiders and snakes. They put us in cages where we existed in our own excrement for hours. It felt like forever.

The first time I remember being raped was at one of the cult ceremonies. I was lying on my back on an altar. My hands and my feet were tied down. There was some kind of ritual going on, a lot of killing, sacrificing of babies. They removed some hearts and put pieces of these hearts in my mouth and up my vagina and painted some stuff on the front of me in blood. Then, the first person to rape me was my father. Several other men raped me after him.

My father had a wild-eyed look. I think he was drugged. I felt like I was being stabbed to death. It was terribly painful, like having your insides ripped out.

There were lots of people watching. This was one of the outdoor rituals. The coven that my father was involved with would hook up with people from other cults or other covens. People from different cults would be in different-colored robes. These rituals where I was being raped were on a pretty regular monthly basis.

You had to learn not to feel. You had to be quiet or they'd torture you. My sister was always with me, but sometimes they would not let us be together. I think, frankly, the worst of this whole thing was watching my sister being abused. I just wanted to save her.

At the end of every ritual we went through a process of being hypnotized to forget. We'd wake up in the morning with no memory of what had happened. We'd go along living a very normal life. I would get up and go to school the next day. I do recall feeling exhausted and sometimes spacey. And there was always the fear. That's the one thing that was constant from the time this abuse started: always the fear. I was always afraid.

The fear sometimes took the form of stomachaches. I had night terrors and sleepwalked around the house. I would wake up and I would be standing someplace in the house. I later learned that sleep disturbances are frequently a part of any kind of post-trauma reaction.

My father was an alcoholic. From the time that this abuse started, he was in and out of hospitals with extreme panic attacks. At the time, they didn't know what was wrong. They would hospitalize him for long, long periods. Then he would come home and try to go back to work. The abuse would stop during the periods of time when he was in the hospital. I recall feeling terrified that he would die. I felt like it was my fault that he was sick.

When I was about ten, we moved to a new house and my mother went back to work. My father was a construction worker. He hardly worked at all and the rape at home escalated. My father was probably coming into my room once a week. He would also drug me at home with some form of tranquilizer. He would come in and say, "Here, take this pill." He would say horrible things. He would call me names, call me a whore. He would make me have oral sex with him.

When I started my period at thirteen, it was a terrifying experience for me, because of the blood. I had no idea why, but I remember the summer I started my period, I was close to having a psychotic break. That was the first sign that I was having serious trouble. I was extremely hyper-vigilant. I would go around at night locking all the windows as soon as the sun would go down. Lots of fears just ransacking my mind. But I had no idea why. My mother did what mothers did back then: she took me to the pediatrician, who said, "She worries too much." The cult abuse stopped shortly after I got my period and the abuse at home stopped, too.

We were very lucky—they threw us out of the cult because my

father became such a loose cannon at that point. I think they were sure that they had us well enough under control that we wouldn't remember. My father was always drunk, really falling apart. They started psychiatrically hospitalizing him.

I was a very, very, very depressed teenager. My sister was the perfect little girl. Never made a wave, never did anything wrong. My sister and I differed in that as I got into my middle teens— fourteen, fifteen, sixteen—I became rebellious. I got very political as a teenager growing up in the late 60s and did some acting out. Certainly nothing like the ways kids act out now. I cut school but I remained a straight-A student. I figured out exactly how many days I could miss and still pass. I started experimenting with drinking and smoking pot and liked it, but it didn't become a problem until later.

I started getting into raging arguments with my father at home. All I knew was that I hated him. He was always drunk. He was barely working. When I got involved with the boy who became my first husband, my father started laying down ridiculous rules. We got into screaming matches and I challenged his authority on everything.

As a teenager, I was dead sexually. I don't remember having any sexual feelings. I didn't go through that stage of becoming a woman where you get excited about it. I was always terrifically ashamed or embarrassed when anyone talked about sex. My first kiss was when I was sixteen and that was kind of exciting. Just before I turned seventeen, I fell absolutely head over heels in love with my first husband. We were good kids in that sense. We did not have intercourse until we got married. I was eighteen and desperate to get out of the house.

My mother finally left my father right after I got married because of my father's alcoholism. She had been planning to leave him for years, but stayed for me. She had intended to wait until my sister had graduated from high school but just couldn't hang on anymore. At that point my father went on Social Security and just drank constantly.

Right after my mother left him, I felt compelled to try to save him and to try to make sure he wouldn't kill himself. I would come home from nursing school and my husband would be drinking. Then my drunk father would start calling me and telling me he was going to kill himself. I did that for a while but got really fed up. Finally, I stopped having any contact with him at all. He was disgusting; he was a drunk.

I started having a lot of anxiety as soon as I got married. I didn't know it was about the sex. That consciousness developed later in the marriage. I was in nursing school and witnessing a lot of surgeries. So between having sex and watching the blood and guts at the hospital, memories were being triggered all over the place. I didn't understand what was happening at the time. The only thing I experienced was chronic massive anxiety: shaking, hyperventilating, feeling dizzy, and a constant gnawing in the pit of my stomach.

I was very good at hiding it. I didn't know it was anxiety. I had no emotional or psychological sophistication at all. I thought there was something physically wrong with me. So I started going to doctors who would do tests and tell me there was nothing wrong with me except that I worried too much.

Six months into my marriage, I fell. It was a very minor sort of fall, but my back went into spasm and it never stopped. I had to drop out of nursing school because of the constant physical pain in my back. Pain is also part of the cult programming. Rather than having the memory emerge, what will happen is some part of your body will go into pain. It's distraction. I understand that chronic pain and lots of accidents are very common among cult survivors.

I never slept. I was always shaking; I was often frightened. I had weird dizzy sensations. I was feeling very spacey. I was terrified. I thought I had some kind of strange disease. I kept looking through my nursing books trying to find a disease that would fit my symptoms. Later, I learned I had an agitated depression. If you are in that state, you can't sleep at all. You're constantly anxious. You can't stop the anxiety. I stayed in bed for about a year.

My orthopedic doctor could not find out what was wrong with me. He sent me to a psychiatrist who, in the first session, gave me Valium and told me that if I didn't feel better in twenty minutes, I should take another one. He gave me codeine and Darvon for my back and chloral hydrate to sleep. I felt better immediately. An average dose of Valium is maybe ten milligrams a day. I started taking over 100 milligrams a day immediately and all I felt was normal. I had been completely nonfunctional for a year. And on all this stuff, I could function. I felt normal! I wasn't frightened all the time. I could focus. I went back to school. I just loved it, it was like a godsend.

I had no idea that these drugs were addicting. They were given to me as completely non-habit-forming, nonaddictive, no-problem drugs. This started my seven-year addiction to prescription drugs which, over time, got worse. At the same time, the chronic pain stuff stayed, got worse, it moved into my neck and my head. I started going from doctor to doctor to doctor looking for a solution to the pain I was having.

I became aware at some point during this period that I was using the pain as an excuse not to have sex. I didn't understand that. My husband was supporting me as best he could. He would take me to the doctors. He wasn't abusive in any way.

The bottom came after I had been referred to a doctor who did some unnecessary and rather damaging jaw surgery that was supposed to help the pain I was in. I knew that I was addicted to these drugs. I'd been through withdrawals. I knew that the drugs were the only things that helped. I would go to a doctor, he'd prescribe for a while, I'd get strung out, he'd yank the prescription, and then I'd go through withdrawal again. This doctor who did the jaw surgery became my last and final connection. He gave me what I wanted, in the amounts I wanted, and refilled my prescription without question. I did nothing. I was trying to recover from the jaw surgery and I just used drugs around the clock. I never left my house. I stopped eating. I did want to die.

I thought about killing myself a lot. I used to carve on my arms with a knife. I just wanted to die and I was playing with suicide. Self-mutilation is very, very common with incest survivors. It can be a way, especially if the memories are repressed, to make sense out of the pain. You know, you cut yourself, you feel pain, and there's a concrete reality to it. It's also a way to deal with the psychic numbing that goes on. You actually feel something.

At the end of two years after this surgery, I was overdosing constantly. I weighed sixty-five pounds. My tongue was black from malnutrition. I hadn't had very much contact with my mother and when she saw me she flipped. She demanded that I do something. And through a series of events which I believe were divinely inspired, I was hospitalized psychiatrically.

The beginning was hard. I was trying to make a decision about whether or not I wanted to live. I made a suicide attempt in the hospital; I slit my wrist. After that attempt, things really opened up for me. On some level, although it wasn't conscious yet, I wanted to try and stay alive. There was one person in particular, I call her my first angel, at the hospital. She was an aide who spent hours talking to me. She introduced me to an inner world of feelings and senses that I had no idea existed. I was given permission for the first time in my life to have a feeling, to verbalize my feelings. It was thrilling. I stayed in that hospital for several months and it gave me my beginning. I filed for divorce while I was in there. I knew that there was no way I could stay off drugs if I went back to my husband.

I left the hospital and went back on drugs real fast. And I was out of control again within a few months. At that point, I decided that the drugs were really a problem. I put myself in a drug recovery program. They introduced me to AA. Although I hadn't lived the same kind of lifestyle as the people in there had, I identified with their feelings. That was my introduction to the program. And to therapy.

I did all the ACA work, but something was still gnawing away at me. I had a hard time staying sober. I kept relapsing. I kept getting up to about two and a half years and I would always relapse. I understand now it was a way to keep the memories down. Every time they got close, I relapsed.

I was in therapy and recovery for a long time before these memories surfaced. The first real memory surfaced only about four years ago, when I was thirty-five. I was in a therapy session. It was a couple session. I had just gotten married a second time and was having a tremendously difficult time in the marriage.

I was having a lot of trouble with sex. We were in a session with a therapist who has made a huge difference in my life—I was in therapy with her for ten years—so I really trusted her. In the middle of the session, in discussing some of the sexual troubles I was having, I had a thought. I thought of my father and I thought of sex in the same second. A shot of electricity went through my body, like a rush of fear.

I was a therapist at the time and I knew enough to say something to my therapist. I said, "This weird thing just happened. I don't know what's going on here, probably nothing, but I just thought of sex and thought of my father in the same thought and I had this jolt of fear." She asked me to focus on the fear. And all I can tell you is that it was like all hell broke loose inside. I began to feel nauseous. I thought I was going to throw up. There was fear charging through my body at an unimaginable level. I started feeling like I was going to pass out. It was unbelievable what was happening in my body. I put my head down between my legs and said, "I'm going to pass out." I lay on the floor and she was asking me to just stay with it. I had done a lot of very deep work with her so I was willing to do that. My mind was going insane. I got into a fetal position and then suddenly I knew where I was . . . I was four years old, in my bed at home, on my side, and my father was in bed with me. I could feel it in my body. I was in shock, shock and terror.

Right before this first memory emerged for me, my sister had started going to Adult Children of Alcoholics meetings. We were talking for the first time in our entire lives. I asked her if she had any memories of being molested, but she thought no. For a while I only had this one memory and I believed that the abuse had only happened one time. Then, my sister began to have memories of being abused by my father at home, too.

My sister really fell to pieces. I went to stay with her for a while. All of a sudden she had memories flying out. There was no control over them; no containment. The first night I was there, she told me that she had had a memory of being in the mountains at a lodge with my father and all of our family friends, of being in a room with them all molesting her. As a therapist, I understood how memories emerge; I knew that people don't make this stuff up. I still sat there with my sister and thought, "She's out of her mind. She has completely lost it. There's no way this happened. She's having a psychotic episode." I just didn't believe that there was any reality to it.

When I went to bed that night, it suddenly occurred to me that as my sister had been talking, I had been seeing pictures of a room in my head—which I hadn't given any thought to. I suddenly thought, "What if I'm seeing the same room?" The next morning I got out two pieces of paper. I said to my sister, "You go over there and draw the room. I'm going to draw it, too. Let's see if they match." They were identical. Where we had the people standing was identical. The layout of the room was identical. I could not see my sister and she could not see me. I was on the bed and she was on the floor next to me.

Then the cult memories started to emerge. Having my sister there has been such a blessing, because I think even as I'm telling you my story, especially with the cult stuff, there's a part of me that says, "This couldn't have happened. How could this have happened?" If my sister had not been remembering the same stuff separately, I would think I was some kind of lunatic.

The memories are still coming. Last week, I had a memory of being in a cage. I was bound; my arms, my legs, and my head were bound to the cage by a leather strap so I couldn't move. I had vomited on myself—they gave me something that made me vomit, they also gave me something that made me go to the bathroom as some form of a purification ceremony. I remember hanging there for hours. I haven't completed that memory but I'm sure there is some sort of ritual that comes after this. This is a horrific process my therapist and I go through. It's easier now. In the beginning it was horrible.

I feel lots of different things about my father today. I pity him. I hold him accountable, absolutely. I hate what he did. I think the hardest thing in this is the ambiguity of it because my father was a very damaged man and the abuser was not all that he was. He was a pretty lousy father but I can remember moments of genuine kindness from him. It was in him. I have had days where I am just enraged that he fucking died. It seems like he gets out of everything. What I would wish for my father is that he would fully realize the impact of what he did. All this taken so much from me.

My God! —I couldn't feel joy for so many years of my life; I lost so many years. I lost the ability to go through a day and enjoy it; I lost my innocence, and my ability to trust; I lost my ability to feel safe in the world; my ability to laugh was gone for years; I lost my ability to have intimate relationships and to have sexual relationships without fear. I still don't know what that's like. I'm beginning to learn. Just beginning. I'm learning how to live with these things through the principles of the program; what happens to my father is up to God.

All of this has also given me a lot: compassion, the ability to truly understand what it's like to suffer. I guess maybe the most important thing I've learned is not to blame the victim. Our society just loves to do that. It's given me a strength that I don't think most people know. The best gift of all is the ability to help other people who have experienced similar things. It's the only thing that gives meaning and worth to what I went through.

I really have been seeing the light from the beginning of my recovery. It was very small at first. I've done so much grieving and it's still hard now in the midst of this process. I love my life today. I love my work. I have the most incredible support system; friends now that I've had for many, many years. I can laugh now. I still go through weeks where I'm depressed and I can't feel any joy and my laugh feels hollow. It pisses me off. Sometimes I feel like they are still taking it from me.

But there is such excitement getting to the very bottom and uncovering all of it so you can finally let it go. It's a relief, in a way. I used to say to my first therapist that there was too much pain here for what I knew about my life. It didn't make sense. Now it makes sense. All of it makes sense. When things like this happen, you think, "Why me?" I think the answer is that it can happen to anybody.

When I think about the cult today, I think that every single time I'm kind, every single time I'm able to love someone or give to them, I defy those assholes. I think they're as evil as anybody can get. Our society is where we were thirty or forty years ago regarding incest in terms of denial of ritual abuse. The only way any of this stuff comes out into the light is because survivors are willing to talk about it—even in the face of ridicule and disbelief and a questioning of their motives.

There is a way out. There are people who will help and there is a loving God who will guide you out. All you have to do is ask.

We shall not cease from exploration
And the end of all our exploring
Will be to arrive where we started
And know the place for the first time.

T. S. ELIOT
Four Quartets

EPILOGUE

$\mathcal{I}$F after reading these stories you have identified with anyone and have seen yourself or parts of yourself in them, you now know that there is a way out. The cycle of abuse can and must be stopped. It can stop with you.

After all the hours of conversation with each person interviewed, I have come to realize that no one is to blame. That is the difficult part. Forgiveness is a process of understanding. The abuser is almost always acting out a conscious or unconscious part of his own past. Sometimes it is impossible to get to the actual source because the legacy goes back so many generations. I remember being struck by this thought while watching the movie *My Left Foot*. I saw the imprint of the Irish father, so out of touch with his feelings, taught by generations of well-meaning teachers that men and boys do not show affection, emotion, or love. In this movie I saw the imprint of my own Irish grandfather, obviously taught by his father, who was taught by his father and so on and so on. Because of this legacy, I was raised by my father in an atmosphere devoid of communication. Feelings and emotions were never discussed. No wonder generations on my father's side drank alcohol to be able to remove the pain of never being able to express themselves. Hundreds of years later my father drank alcoholically and I was a victim of that legacy.

Now, what if my forefathers had been as physically abusive as Randy Shilts's mother, or Gary Crosby's father, or Traci Lords's father? What was the pain? Where was this behavior learned? Most likely from their own legacies. Cheryl Crane, B. J. Thomas, and Dr. Richard Berendzen were sexually abused. But what about their abusers? Were they also abused?

Piece together the stories from your parents' childhoods. With your growing understanding from your adult viewpoint, you can begin to have compassion for their pain. In doing so, blame will slowly dissolve. John Bradshaw says, "As a parent myself, I feel accountable for the things I've done to my children. I have come to realize that there were ways in which I wasn't there for them. I have asked their forgiveness for things I did and didn't do. I have also been confronted by my children and have acknowledged the truth of what they have said."

Sometimes I've thought of blaming *my* parents to explain any failings I might have as a mother, but that's just a way of minimizing my own role in my behavior to my son. The cycle of abuse may be passed on, abusing parents may be victims themselves, but their victims still need to have amends made to them. Parents are accountable to their children regardless of the abuse in their own pasts.

Unfortunately, amends cannot always be made. Some parents may die before any confrontation can occur. And some parents choose to remain in denial, leaving the abused child to work it out on his or her own.

It's hard to forgive. For some people it is impossible. But to forgive frees you of the burden of your anger. The abuser has taken such an emotional toll from you already. Why let them take more? If you have problems today, the patterns that created them began a long time ago.

You can break the cycle. You can change the imprint of your past. Your children and future generations of your family do not have to inherit the sadness, the anger, the pain, the violence, the shame, the humiliation, and the confusion.

Feel good about yourself. You survived. You have chosen not to be a victim any longer. The worst is over.

Through reading these stories we've seen the importance of facing the anger, of going back and reliving a painful past to understand it. It is necessary to do the work on oneself to get through this process. Be patient. It takes time—sometimes a lifetime. But along the way there are constant breakthroughs, insights, and understanding. It is an exciting process, an ongoing process of emotional development and spiritual growth.

I have found (and have had this confirmed by my friends in the health-care field) that once I was able to piece together the puzzle of my own childhood, I was able to understand myself and why I acted out the way I did. I finally understood it wasn't my fault and it wasn't my father's fault. We were both victims of patterns of behavior passed on for generations.

The double impact of this information is that it applies to all people. Whenever I see a juvenile delinquent on television being admonished for his inexplicable behavior, I am able to look beyond. What happened in this child's life to make him act out in such horribly inappropriate ways? Why does he appear to be unfeeling? What happened to him that made feeling anything so painful that to survive he tuned out and turned his feelings off? Who is to blame? The child? Those who raised the child? Or those who raised the parents who raised that child? You see, the beat goes on. No one is to blame. It is too deep, too buried to point the finger. This is not to minimize what happened to you. It is important not to forget. Remembering keeps us vigilant.

We have a tremendous opportunity in our generation. Through the information now available, the breakthroughs in the medical field, and the quest of our psychiatrists, psychologists, therapists, social workers, and those who have a passionate desire to unravel the secrets of the human condition, we can begin to change the behaviors that are negative, destructive, and abusive.

John Bradshaw says, "As children, we idealize our parents and we develop a compulsion to protect them. We break that compulsion when we face the truth of our past. It is very hard to do. We have to go against the terrors of our earliest childhood. But if we don't, the compulsion to protect the parent generates the same mistakes they made, which are then carried on from generation to generation. As we end old repetitions, the courage arises to risk new behavior—more valuing, more democratic. This will improve the quality of life for us all."

There is now a new consciousness, a circle of thought recognizing parenting as our most important job. Children need to be nurtured and valued; no child *ever* deserves to be beaten, abused, or violated; children deserve our trust. When we have learned that, Wednesday's Children will no longer be full of woe, but filled with the pleasure and wonder of their individual purity and innocence.

CURRENT STATISTICS
COMPILED BY CHILD HELP CENTER

1. In 1990, 2.5 million cases of child abuse and neglect were reported in the United States.
2. This represents an increase of 4% in the last year, 31% in the last five years, and a 117% increase in the last decade.
3. The average age of the reported child victims was 7.2 years of age.
4. Over three children die each day from child abuse (1211 per year). Since 1985, the number of reported child-abuse fatalities has increased over 38%. Over 50% of the children were less than one year of age at the time of death. These figures most likely represent the lowest estimate of the problem.
5. In over 80% of reported cases, the perpetrator is known to the child or is the child's parent.
6. Of the reported cases of child abuse and neglect, 27% involve physical abuse, 15% involve sexual abuse, 46% involve neglect, and 9% involve emotional abuse.
7. Approximately 53% of reported cases of child abuse and neglect were substantiated in 1986. Through 1990, substantiated reports average over 40%. Substantiation figures vary from state to state, depending on each state's definition of a substantiated report.
8. For every 1000 children in America, thirty-nine are reported being abused or neglected.
9. The consequences of physical abuse are far greater for younger

children. Children from infancy to age five are 28% of the general population of abused children, but sustain a disproportionatley high 74% of fatalities. While the average age of children in all child-abuse reports is 7.2, the average age of fatalities from child abuse is 2.6.

10. Based on studies which show that 25%–35% of women and 10%–20% of men in the United States were victims of sexual abuse as children, it is estimated that over 40 million people, or at least one in six Americans, have been sexually abused.

11. As many as one in three girls and one in five boys will be sexually abused before they turn eighteen years of age.

12. In 1990, approximately 376,000 children were reported as sexually abused.

13. In 1990, approximately 677,000 children were reported as physically abused.

14. Males are eleven times more likely than females to be molested out of the home.

15. About two in three Americans (64%) think they can personally help prevent child abuse. Those who feel most effective include persons under the age of fifty-five, parents of children under eighteen, blacks, and hispanics.

16. A majority of Americans (61%) say they cannot imagine a hypothetical situation when they would approve of a public school teacher hitting a student. This is a marked increase over the 51% who shared this opinion in a survey in 1968. As of early 1990, twenty states had banned corporal punishment in the public elementary and high schools, nine had legislation pending, and thirteen reported active lobbying efforts underway.

17. Over 90% of the public agrees that all elementary schools should offer instruction that teaches children to protect themselves from child abuse, especially sexual abuse.

18. Alcohol is almost always involved in family violence. Up to 80% of all cases involve drinking, whether before, during or after the critical incident.

19. Findings of incest in alcoholic homes were indicated in recent studies of 200 adult children of alcoholics. Almost 30% of the

females in this survey reported some incestuous relationships, typically with fathers and stepfathers.

20. Alcoholism programs identify emotional neglect by parents as a major theme of life for children in alcoholic homes.

21. One out of every thirteen children with a substance-abusing parent is seriously abused each year.

22. According to a recent study, stepdaughters are six times more likely to be sexually abused than daughters who live with a natural father.

23. Recent research states that stepdaughters are five times more likely to be sexually abused by men other than a father or stepfather, especially friends of their parents.

24. There are an estimated 28 million children of alcoholics.

25. Children of alcoholics are three to four times more likely to become alcoholic than children reared by non-alcoholics.

26. Intervention with new parents before the downward spiraling parent-child cycles of abuse are established is a more effective prevention plan than trying to break abusive cycles after they are established. Research shows that the earlier intervention occurs, to support, monitor, and redirect high-risk parents, the greater are the odds of success.

27. The number of children in substitute care increased by nearly 30% nationwide between 1986 and 1989. In Washington, DC, prenatal substance abuse generated a 58% increase in the number of children placed in foster care by the courts.

28. Of the forty-eight states who have provided funding information, twenty-one (42%) received an increase in their 1989 child welfare budgets. The vast majority of these increases merely reflected a cost of living increase. A greater number (twenty-four) reported no change or a decline in revenues.

29. Every fifteen seconds a woman will be abused by her husband and/or boyfriend.

30. Two to four thousand women are beaten to death annually.

31. Twenty-five percent of all women's suicide attempts are preceded by a prior history of battering.

32. More than 50% of all married women will be assaulted at least

once during their marriage. More than 33% of women will be repeatedly assaulted during their marriage.

33. Battery is the single major cause of injury to women.
34. Ten women a day are killed by their partners.
35. In 75% of the states in this country, it is legal for husbands to rape their wives.
36. One person is raped every six minutes.
37. As much as ten times as many rapes occur as are reported.
38. One in three women under the age of fifty can expect to be raped in her lifetime.
39. Half of all rapes are acquaintance rape. Half of all rapes involve a victim, a perpetrator, or both who are teenagers. Of this 50%, up to 80% of raped teenagers are acquaintance-rape victims.

RESOURCE INFORMATION

For information on treatment for addictions or problems related to dysfunctional families, look in your telephone book. You may also call or write to the organizations listed below for hotline counseling, referrals to services in your area, or informational and educational materials.

Alcoholics Anonymous—General Service Office (AA)
475 Riverside Drive, 11th Floor
New York, NY 10115
(212) 870-3440

American Association for Marriage and Family Therapy
1717 K Street, N.W.
Washington, DC 20006
(202) 429-1825

Anorexics/Bulimics Anonymous (ABA)
P.O. Box 112214
San Diego, CA 92111
(619) 685-3344

Batterers Anonymous (BA)
BA Press
8485 Tamarind Ave., Suite D

313

Fontana, CA 92335
(714) 355-1100

Children of Alcoholics Foundation
P.O. Box 4185
Grand Central Station
New York, NY 10163-4185
(212) 754-0656

Cocaine Anonymous—World Service Office, Inc.
3740 Overland Ave., Suite H
Los Angeles, CA 90034-6337
(800) 347-8998

Co-Dependents Anonymous (CODA)
P.O. Box 6292
Phoenix, AZ 85261
(602) 277-7991

DARE America
(800) 223-3273

Incest Survivors Resource Network, International, Inc.
P.O. Box 7375
Las Cruces, NM 88006-7375
(505) 521-4260

National Asian Pacific Families
Against Substance Abuse (NAPAFASA)
420 East 3rd Street, Suite 909
Los Angeles, CA 90013
(213) 617-8277

National Association of Anorexia Nervosa
and Associated Disorders (ANAD)
P.O. Box 7

Highland Park, IL 60611
(708) 831-3438

National Association of Children of Alcoholics (NACOA)
11426 Rockville Pike, Suite 100
Rockville, MD 20852
(301) 468-0985

National Association of Lesbian and
Gay Alcoholism Professionals (NALGAP)
204 West 20th Street
New York, NY 10011
(212) 713-5074

National Child Abuse Hotline
Childhelp USA
P.O. Box 630
Hollywood, CA 90028
(800) 4-A-CHILD (800-422-4453)

National Institute of Drug Abuse (NIDA)
11426 Rockville Pike
Rockville, MD 20852
Information Office: (301) 443-6245
For Help: (800) 662-HELP (800-662-4357)

National Runaway Hotline
(800) 621-4000

Native American Association for
Children of Alcoholics (NANACOA)
P.O. Box 18736
Seattle, WA 98118

Overeaters Anonymous—National Office
P.O. Box 92870

Los Angeles, CA 90009
(800) 743-8703

Parents Anonymous—National Office
520 S. Lafayette Park Place, Suite 316
Los Angeles, CA 90057
(800) 421-0353

Sex Addicts Anonymous
P.O. Box 3038
Minneapolis, MN 55403
(612) 339-0217

Sex and Love Addicts Anonymous (SLAA)
(The Augustine Fellowship)
P.O. Box 119
New Town Branch
Boston, MA 02258
(617) 332-1845

Sexaholics Anonymous
P.O. Box 300
Simi Valley, Ca 93062
(805) 831-3343

Survivors of Incest
Anonymous (SIA)
P.O. Box 21817
Baltimore, MD 21222
(301) 282-3400

Suzanne Somers Institute
. . . For the Effects of Addictions on Families
340 South Farrell Drive, Suite A203
Palm Springs, CA 92262
Affiliate Service Providers
(800) 723-HOPE

Victims of Incest Can Emerge
Survivors in Action (VOICES)
Voices in Action, Inc.
P.O. Box 148309
Chicago, IL 60614
(312) 327-1500

Women for Sobriety
Box 618
Quakertown, PA 18951
(215) 536-8026

ABOUT SUZANNE SOMERS

Throughout the 70s she starred as "Chrissy" in the hit television series "Three's Company." She is the author of a book of poetry, *Touch Me,* published in 1973, and of *Keeping Secrets,* published in 1989. She lectures around the country on behalf of the Children of Alcoholics movement, and is founder and director of the Suzanne Somers Institute . . . For the Effects of Addictions on Families, in Palm Springs, California. In 1991, she produced and starred in the movie *Keeping Secrets,* based on her autobiography, and is currently starring in the hit ABC television series "Step by Step." She continues to lecture throughout the United States and was recently awarded the Distinguished Achievement Award for Public Service from the Secretary of Health and Human Services, Dr. Louis Sullivan. She performs regularly in Las Vegas and Europe with her stage show and was named Las Vegas Entertainer of the Year in 1987. She is happily married to Alan Hamel, her husband of fifteen years, and has one son, Bruce, and two stepchildren, Leslie and Stephen.